Let's Get Dogs#!t

Let's Get Dogs#!t

TOMMY HAWKINS

To order additional copies of this book, contact:
Xlibris LLC
0-800-056-3182
www.xlibrispublishing.co.uk
Orders@xlibrispublishing.co.uk
521391

This book was wrote on the road whilst intoxicated
on a number of things I can't quite remember, so
Critics have mercy
Snobs tone down a sec
Readers have fun

OOO GET Little Intro GET:

This is a true life story about how two friends meet and embark on a journey that will change their lives forever. The contents of this story contains very strong language and obscene behavior, containing a lot of sex and drugs. Matty and Tommy, the real names of Noah and Oscar, met on a Greek island Corfu in 2006. On this island Corfu there is a small town in the south called Kavos, which can only be described as a British brothel that stinks of rotten rat shit. Tommy worked in Kavos for three summers running, and at the end of his last summer in 2008 is when he met Matty for the first time, properly. They both knew of each other but never met other than drunken staff parties until that late summer in 2008. Matty got a job where Tommy was working but unfortunately was filling Tommy's position as he was going home, due to liver and kidney damage. After spending only one week working together, Tommy went home keeping in touch with Matty's antics on Facebook. Two years later Tommy returned to Kavos for a short holiday, and this is where he and Matty met once again, to discuss a trip that was only a drunken fantasy at the time, until a few months later became reality. The first time Tommy and Matty met on their home turf (London, England), was at Heathrow airport on the way to Australia, so this should give you an idea of how much they knew about each other, basically fuck all. Nevertheless, what they did know is that, they are awesome at getting absolute

'Dogs#!t' together (drunk) and the fact that there is never a dull moment when these two mess heads get together. A lot of people who knew Tommy and Matty from Kavos thought this trip was a bad idea for them both, as they are as bad as each other. However Tommy and Matty both knew that this was fate that led them here, and that backpackers around Australia needed these party starters. Before you read on, there is a word in their journal that is used a lot and would like to give you an idea of what it means. It was Matty who introduced this word to the backpacking world, and now everyone uses it. The word is GET. Now GET can be used in any situation or sentence, for example, "Fuck me look at that girl she's a bit GET", "I want to GET GETTED tonight", or simply "just GET". If you still don't understand, don't worry you will, you little GET.

Matty and Tommy thought it would be funny to change their names before they got to Australia. Tommy chose Oscar and Matty chose Noah; however they don't really use these names as much as they wanted, probably because they got absolute 'Dogs#!t' and forgot. The story of Oscar and Noah will be copied word for word out of their journal, with a few minor changes. Tommy's entries will be as normal font and Matty's in *Italic*.

Journal 1

Dear journal. That will be the last time I say dear journal as its too old skool and gay. We left Heathrow at 9pm, after 12 hours of Matty eating everything on the plane; we arrived at Shanghai at 5pm. We sat and waited in this derelict airport for 5 hours. Matty was strumming away on his guitar, when some Chinese girl asked if he would play at a party coming up that weekend somewhere in China. Unfortunately we had another 14 hour flight to catch to Melbourne. 'So sorry my Asian friend we are on route to get Dogs#!t' down under'. Onboard this flight me and Matty began to get 'Dogs#!t' due to free booze and the fact it was New Year's Eve. At midnight me, Matty, two English dudes and one Japanese guy celebrated the end of 2010 and had a good drink for the start of 2011. The stewardesses politely told us to keep the noise down and that if we wanted to carry on drinking to get to the back of the plane. Fortunately for us, the back of the plane is where the booze was kept, happy days.

Oh hello Melbourne, New Year's Day baby! Got a taxi to base hostel where we plan to stay for a few nights until we find a cheaper hostel. Checked into a 10 bedded dorm with some crazy Aussie lads from Queensland and a few English boys, one who is barman downstairs. We went and had a good walk around St. Kilda, proper mental place; everyone's getting on it, happy days. That night in Base hostels bar, we bumped into Matty-Lee a guy we knew from Kavos, proper random. We had a few buckets and jugs, went out after but not a crazy one, still jet lagged.

Sunday woke up early, got a bus pass and went into the city on a tram. Which was pointless paying for as there are no inspectors and you can just walk on. Had a Hungry Jacks (Australia's Burger King) which was good, got back to St. Kilda and got sun burnt on the beach in half hour whilst it was raining. Got back to the hostel for a little siesta before going out. Woke up and had a jug of snakebite, bar closed, nothing open, early night. Woke up early Monday 3rd Jan and had to move as we only booked two nights at Base and there was no more room at the inn. Jumped on a tram not knowing where we were going, jumped off a mile down the road as fate led us to our new home. Booked in for a week at hostel Coffee Palace, glad we did as it's cheaper and feels more like backpacking.

Walked to the beach and brought a Frisbee, we chilled on the beach before finding a cool off license which was also a bar. We were proper baffled, could not get our heads around the fact that you could walk in the offy, buy a six pack, and then sit at a table just simply get pissed and people watch the world go by. On the way back to the room Matty knocked a tray of glasses out of some waitress's hands, classic, definatly one for the journal.

Hey it's Mat here!! Toms having the biggest sleep in the world as we keep going out when all the bars are closing, so I refuse to go to sleep. I nearly bought a skateboard today but thought better of it after some debate, ha-ha. Sitting in the room full of random people wondering where they're all going and what they're all doing tonight . . . . Sting is keeping everyone alive. I love my life, beginning of the best trip ever and only day three. Music has just been turned up in the common room, 'Let's Get Dogs#!t'!!!

After a nice sleep and a pack of six Carlton Draught we took a walk and ended up paying five bucks to get into nothing other than a tranny bar, if we didn't pay to get in we probably would have walked out, but stayed and had the best night yet. I left a bit earlier than Mat, because of a lady boy chatting me up, only to find a 20 man brawl in our hostel over a pizza. Woke up in the morning and found Matty asleep on the sofa in the common room as he went home with some fat Swedish bird. We then got a tram into the city to open our new Aussie banks, then had an amazing smoothie from Boost, then walked to Federation Square and watched the funniest juggler/magician let a 6 year old throw knifes at him. Got back to the room and had a 12 hour sleep (please jet leg fuck off). Woke up bright and early to discover our hostel gives out free pancakes. GET. Then spent a few hours down the beach power tanning and getting good at Frisbee. Looking forward to a Thai curry tonight with an old friend Alex who I met in Kavos 5 years ago, it's her birthday.

So we got a little bit 'Dogs#!t' before going to the curry house more than anticipated and ended up being like 40 mins late, but it was worth the funny walk on the longest road ever, then after much debate broke 1 of our rules by getting a cab to the place, because we were walking the other direction, ha-ha. "But its ok I know this place like the back of my hand". Before I go on I think I better explain our "rules" to you. Me and Tommy both agreed on certain rules such as—no planes, no cabs and no haircuts so far only fucked one up, let's see how long the others last for! Finally got there, took our shoes off, and met Alex and her friends. Sat down with 2 bottles of wine for me and Tom and had loads of starters and 2 Thai red curries that were really nice but not that hot☹. Alex and her friends where really cool, so cool in fact that we got a lift home with them which was really lucky, as we would never have got home thinking about it now.

At this moment in time I'm finding it hard to write since I'm now faced with Tom and our newly acquired GOON!! The end of the curry night ended up with me and Tom 'Dogs#!t' once again walking into our party hostel playing games we had no idea how to play, but acted like we did. Finally putting ourselves to bed was woken up by the Scottish lads because 1 of them ended up in a fight (bloody wimps), they were moaning for ages, but was funny as they woke up the angry German who was sleeping above me and was possibly angry because his girlfriend was sleeping above Tom, so no boning there then, ha-ha. He replied with this almighty "would you guys just shut the fuck up", Scottish "sorry German". Not forgetting 1 Scottish lad got lucky that night, but for the life of me have no idea what the hell he was doing to the poor girl. Hours on end, enough said. Next day got up real early, hit the beach for some more Frisbee and a lot of pancakes, got a bit burnt and was only in the sun for like 2 hours, mega hot. Then fancied an ice cream so thought we would hook up with our ice cream girl, she was awesome making our ice creams massive for a tiny price, legend! Come back with our bellies full of ice cream and met our new roomies. Two girls, finally, they were really cool as well, then not too long after 3 guys from Essex, then shortly after that another girl. Introductions over and jokes flying about me and Tom had our first taste of goon! Was wicked got us fucked! Flew out the door with our new roomies to Base for a night out.

Pretty much already 'Dogs#!t', we all jumped on a tram to Base which was pumping, nearly not getting in for not having any I.D we hit the dance floor. Felt sorry for Kavos buddy Matty-Lee working in Base whilst me and Noah was getting on it. After Mat come second place in a wet-t-shirt competition (which got us a week's stay at any Base hostel in Oz) and a serious pole dance off, we had to leave because I got chucked out for pretty much fuck all. On the way home we took another wise short cut, which this time actually worked. Got back to the hostel, me, Lucy and the Essex boys played some foosball while Matty was getting not so lucky with Chloe. SHIT!! We woke up late for our day trip to the Great Ocean Road, managed to grab what we could to make the coach. Really cool day out seeing, Koala bears, Kangaroos, Bells Beach (from movie Point Break), Lighthouse (from kids TV show round the twist), rainforests and loads of beautiful rocks (12 opostals). 14 hours later back at the hostel with goon.

After a couple of glasses of goon had an early night, starting to wake up a bit later. Got up around 10am to have breakfast, Tom couldn't eat all of his so I helped out then immediately regretted it. Went to Base to claim my wet-t-shirt prize, but got told to come back Monday and get it. We will get our free nights fuckers!! Walked back, hit the beach for some more sunbaving and Frisbee, come back and had a nap. Then woke up and started playing drinking games with all the guys in our room with a lot of what is now called special box. Chloe was the first 1 down in ring of fire at 11pm only remembering 1 thing . . . where's Steven lol. As Alex got attached to the name Steven we kept it all night. Oh yeah not forgetting pancake girl, Monique, who didn't get any pancakes in the morning, but got a shit load of songs thrown at her about pancakes. All done in the room we ventured out into the common room where more drinking games took place, but not for long as me and Tom single handedly killed the game for being too drunk. Moved onto the foosball table realising after many dollars we can't play foosball. Everyone got food then went to bed, me and Alex stayed up talking shit, then went to the bakery at like 3am and met some guys Alex met in Vietnam! Weird as hell! I guess that what travelling's about, months apart then meeting up in a bakery, ha-ha.

So we wake up to get our pancakes, (well Mat did, I was still in bed fully clothed), and all was on offer was warm cornflakes. Weather has turned a bit so no sunbaving or Frisbee, just a slow day of packing our bags ready to hit the city to stay with a couple of girls Alex from Kavos and her friend Emily. With our useful Matnav and Tom Tom we found the apartment, which was 26 floors up looking over the city, pukka views. Had a wicked night in our new pad playing ring of fire with special box, proper little rave up. We woke up and got a tram back to St. Kilda to collect Matty's wet-t-shirt prize. Got back to the penthouse and said bye to Alex and Emily, then got to the train station to find out the train was cancelled due to floods and had to get a 12 hour bus ride to Sydney.

After a long uncomfortable journey we arrive at Sydney at 6.30am (it's my birthday, yay). Then not really having a clue where to go, as we still haven't looked at a map yet, we jumped on a tube and a bus to arrive at Bondi Beach. After a few hours walking round trying to find a hostel we found our new home, Noah's Ark Backpackers. Gagging for a beer; we done a mini bar crawl and watched some surfers getting wiped out by some mean ass waves. Then got a few bottles of wine to drink in our room with our new roomies, 2 Danish dudes, 1 Scottish bloke and 2 Brazilian birds. We all then got ready and went down into the bar. 3 or 4 jugs of beer later I (lightweight, as I am) was in bed first. Matty and the others carried onto a bar playing drunken ping pong. We got up and got a bus and a train to the city to collect our new Aussie bank cards which were sent here from Melbourne. Took a walk to see the Harbour Bridge and the Opera House (proper little tourists), then got back to the hostel, had a Thai curry and an early night.

Hello Mr. Diary it's been almost 3 weeks since we last spoke and fuck me a lot has gone on. Just to let you know it's the 30th Jan, I'm in the hostel after a little smoke on the beach with the Essex boys, girl from Finland, girl from Germany and the Swedish lads. Miss Matty he is working for a surf camp, cool new job he has got, I will let him tell you more. I'm not working yet, because I broke my collar bone 2 weeks ago surfing. We have both met so many people, mainly Scandinavians, and have not got a bad thing to say about any of them, they are all awesome. Our room is like the busiest room in the whole hostel, probably because me and Matty invite everyone to play drinking games. Sydney is amazing, so many great days out, like when we all took the bus to the Harbour to chill out in the Royal Botanic Gardens, with a bag of weed to watch the wild bats and cockatoos. Our new home Bondi is so close to the city, and only 20 meters to the beach, I suppose that's why they call it Bondi Beach. FUCK FUCK FUCK I've just got back from the toilet and there's some geezer from Israel running around with a knife, see you soon.

Hello again it's been a few days, getting bad at this diary. It's become groundhog day in Bondi, we wake up either go to the beach, or get a bus somewhere, then buy a box of special stuff drink it on the hostel rooftop, then invite the whole hostel to the beach for a midnight session. A few nights ago I tried having sex with a beached whale but couldn't do anything because of my broken collar bone, I've got jump start cables used as rope to help me get in and out of bed and help in situations like this, but this sicko who was trying to have sex with this poor ginger cripple, could not stop laughing and woke the whole room up.

Why hello there it's been a while since I last wrote something in this diary of justice. I've got a job ☺ couldn't ask for a better job at this moment in time, getting to sell something I love doing. So I've been away from the boys for a week or so at surf camp, it's been so awesome, met some really cool people and can now say I'm a surfer ha-ha! 2 hours south of Sydney is a cool little town called Jeringa, everything a surf camp should be, god the food is wicked. So the week started for me at surf camp as a customer and ended up with me being a worker. All the guys down there were so cool to me, within days felt so comfortable down there. Missed Tommy though as so many things were happening and he wasn't there to see it all, but like brothers we kept in touch on the phone every day, ha-ha. Australia day down there was so funny, went for an early surf, then got on it from like 1pm, got really fucked with the guys at camp chipped my tooth, and walked into a random house with a pack of 6 beers, I tried saying I was Noah from Byron Bay, it didn't work. By the end of the week I was in the water with the guys, teaching people how to surf, so weird but cool. Coming back home from camp was wicked, went to Scu Bar with the guys from surf camp and didn't pay for a thing all night, so you can guess how that ended, like a scene from the hangover. Finally got back to Noah's, give Tommy a big hug, and told him all the mad shit what happened. As soon as me and Tom were re-united, the room got back to its old ways, sex, drugs, rock and roll.

Wot shapnin, so I suppose it's been about a week since we picked up this bible. I've just got back from the city, love Sydney, had a few beers with a couple from Romford, Dagenham Dave's if you ask me, but it was cool to have a bit of banter with some Essex geeks. Missing Matty he is back on surf camp. My arm is slowly getting better, so not long now till I can join him. Had some cool nights out last week, Me, Matty and the 202 massive went on the rooftop for some Vodka and passion pop in watermelon, then headed to the shack to see 2 guitarists live, they were 1 white guy and 1 Chinese guy from Denmark, pretty fucking awesome. Then we all went to the beach, roughly 50 people, 4 guitars and a load of goon, love my life.

So me and Tom noticed there is nothing about me or Kirsa in this book, so we have to change that. My name is Johanna and I am a nice girl. That all about me that you have to know. Tom is drinking every day, all day, almost. But who cares we are having the time of our lives. My writing is horrible, feel like I'm high, but who cares? Matty is on a surf camp and we are missing him, but at least we have the goon, Tom has. Room full of French people, can't understand a shit and there going crazy with a football, wwwaaaaaaa. Ok now they started talking about cars with Eddie, so I'm going to sleep, men are sooo boring, not really, love you all, WHAT IS THIS MADNESS.

Had a really nice day today, woke up had some classic English beans on toast, got myself a few job interviews for tomorrow, then went and watched some waves (the biggest I've ever seen, some reaching 25-30 foot). Bumped into Swedish Jay on the beach and walked to the cliff top to get some good pictures of the waves crashing behind us, then got the German boys to go for a body board. Now just chilling in the room with my goon, French dudes and some Swedish chicks listening to Jack Johnson, getting ready to go to Beaches (awesome bar). Hopefully Matty is home tonight to join us. He is missing some good nights, our room 202 has turned into a fucking nightclub, people on the rooftop come and ask us if there is another party in the room once the rooftop closes, I should start selling tickets. Another sweet day today, woke up early, went swimming then took a walk along the coast with Jay and new friend Duncan from Milton Keynes. We sat on the Cliffside smoke some weed and watched some amazing wave's crash into the rocks, which made rainbows form in the Ocean. Matty still not home, should be home tonight, it's Jay and the Germans last night, so we are all going to Worldz Bar in Kings Cross.

Wow what a night, Worldz Bar is awesome, the music was perfect. Me and Matty turned the dance floor into a mosh pit, never seen Jay so happy, nice little send off for the "dirty fucker's tour". We left the club around 3am trying to find where the bus stop was, not really knowing where we were going, come across a shopping trolley (hours of fun). Finally got back to the hostel, after 2 or 3 pies we went to bed, knowing we had to be up at 8am for our days graft as gardeners. So we woke up and walked about 3 miles to some South African's Mansion, for Noah and Oscars first day of gardening carnage. The guy was loaded, his house was furnished with American White Oak and Marble. We both got 90 bucks each and a lift home. We got back to the hostel and played power hour, or as everyone in 202 calls it goon hour. Pretty much 'Dogs#!t', we all walked to the beach and had a jam with the New Zealand band.

Oi Oi booky boy, it's been a couple of days, and what a mental couple of days it's been. Me, Matty and a group of complete nutters got a bus to good vibrations festival, with no tickets we all managed to sneak in. Matty and April jumped the portaloo's, Duncan and the rest snuck through the fence, not able to climb because my arm is still in a sling, I had to blag some bullshit story to security that I knew the DJ and that I was an important man, gooned up as I was, it worked. I got in just in time to see Phoenix, some sweet house DJ and Faithless. After all splitting up in the festival we all met in Kings Cross for a really funny journey home.

I'm back in the book of justice once again, so its Sunday night, looks like it's going to be a normal party for 202, and yes success it was. So everyone is walking down to the pie shop to grab a pie or 10. Then I find myself without Tom and with the pie man Ash and a Norwegian chick, Eline. 3 pies later me and Eline kind of had drunken silly business, then as we were heading back, we bumped into this guy called Ivan. He was so cool got talking for 2 mins, then he offered me and Eline to come to his for a drugs fest! It was so casual and so funny, after 2 hours of Pixie Dust Ivan was asleep, and me and Eline was hanging, this went on for 18 hours. We talked heaps of bollox, nothing else, just hanging out, was so cool, haven't done that with a girl for some time. My body was so numb, I couldn't move, but wished I had my phone so I could ring Tom and tell him the crazy shit that's happening, like the rainbows kicking in and Ivan waking up for another dance and more drugs, told me he loved me and Eline, then went back to sleep. After having so much of a good thing, we braved the outside world, crossed the road, dodged the funny looking cars and headed to Noah's. Was really funny seeing the others and trying to tell them where we had been.

'Oooh, maybe can I see that a liddle' (sorry book, private joke, it's just a quote from my Danish friend asking for a spliff). So it's been a few more days, got myself a little job "geeettt". Made my first Aussie staircase, not gonna lie it was pretty crap, but what do they expect for 20 bucks an hour. We all went to Beach Road Club last night. Canadian dudes, Swedish chicks, German Dan, Northern girls, Me, Matty and a shit load of goon. Wish I never because I struggled in work today. Going back there tonight because there's been an international skate competition on Bondi Beach today and there is fresh GETS everywhere.

Ay hahh!! So the skate comp, what a day, couldn't believe how good it was, they turned the shitty Bondi Bowl into a well groomed arena. Filled with hot girls to the max, loads of pro skaters, even seen some heroes of mine (Bob Burquist and Bucky Lasik). Was so unreal, it was like I was playing Tony Hawk on the PlayStation again. So after a solid no food diet, we hit the goon hard once more! Went to Beaches, saw a punk band playing in there, but they were so fucking cheesy, it was hilarious, after a while the ozzy punks couldn't play at all. The mosh pit was out of control, with all the skaters going mad, I even saw a guy get knocked out cold, and me and my new moshing buddy's decided to mosh round him. All moshed out and pretty drunk found myself hanging with a bunch of Swedish chicks. They were cool and hot all at the same time, lol. I even got myself a little kiss didn't I! Yes! I blagged it as a skater. Lost Tom and ended up walking home with 4 pies. Got to stop with the pies now.

Ay up ally oopah! Just had my first boy's trip out to a new beach for surf. Feel bad on Tommy though because he had to work. Me, Brad, Phil and Jordan hit the train early to Cronulla beach for a surf day!! After a little nap on the train, we were a short walk from the beach, couldn't wait to get in my wetsuit and get out. Waves were so good in the morning, no people at all, kicked Bondi surf all round. It was good to see all 4 of us ripping, I really surprised myself that's for sure, all starting to click abit now, hard work starting to pay off, well abit of hard work anyway. I grabbed a subway with the boys, had a look round the town, was really nice, got talking to loads of people that were so cool. We headed back out for another surf, but weather had turned abit, then just thought it was best to head home, but a great day with the guys. Finally back at 202 with a bag of weed and loads of goon, 'Dogs#!t' was on the cards again.

Gooday little book, Oscar here! It's been almost a week thought I would say hello. I've been working all week, made some sweet decking and pathway to complete my staircase, made a few hundred bucks as well as Matty who done some laboring, so we are set to go to Byron Bay on March 1st. We have had some fucking awesome nights out this week. The best was when me, Matty, Jordan and Dan all done some Acid trips and sat on the grass in front of Bondi Beach, watching waves, spaceships and wherever our imaginations took us. It was the funniest night yet, the trip, which we called the venga bus from Bondi to Ibiza lasted 12 hours. I just can't explain how fucked we all were, good times. The acid night was a good start to our last weekend in Bondi. After our last messy weekend, Me, Matty, Jordan, Emma, Phoebe, Matilda,

Anna, Corey, Brad and some random Swedish dude all got a 14 hour journey to Byron Bay, it was a bus, train then another bus, long journey but well worth it, gonna miss Bondi.

Wow, Byron Bay is the best place yet. It was a bit of a mission finding a hostel for 10 people, but after a walk around, we found our new home "Main Beach". It's sick, we are a stone's throw away from the beach, kitchen is huge, TV room is massive and the BBQ area backs onto an outdoor pool. After a nice day on the beach, we all started drinking around 4pm, by 10pm we were all drunk and split up in different clubs, me and Anna were in Chunky Monkeys, where I failed miserably at a drinking comp, and Anna won. After getting up early for a run to another beach (need to get fit titty's are getting big), it was cool hearing everyone's stories from the night. Today was another sweet day on the beach, the girls buried Matty in the sand and made him look like an ice cream (very artistic). I brought myself more bracelets, a necklace and an earring all made from wood, hair is getting long, look like a proper hippy now (sweet). We all finally made it out together, went to Coco's for free drink, and then ended up in Chunky Monkeys, really good night. I woke up to discover my drag drags were left on the beach last night. So as me, Matty and Emma walked to another beach, south of Byron, I found my thongs, happy days. Then on the Cliffside before the beach, we see about 15 dolphins all swimming really close to the beach. It was amazing as we got down to the beach, flipper and his friends were literally 5 meters from shore, so as Matty went surfing me and Emma sat and watched them, as the northern girls would say OMG loving life.

A few more days have passed and what a sweet couple of days it's been, it's become a ritual for me to get up and go out for a run and every time see dolphins, I can't keep fit through surfing, still can't swim, not long now I hope, Matty on the other hand is smashing it, proper little surfer, the little GET I'm well jealous, my time will come. I'm a bit stoned right now, Me, Matty and the room 8 crew got a bus to the hippy capital of the world (Nimbin). This town was formed by party going hippies that went to a festival in the 60's, basically built a town after the rave because they didn't want to go back to reality and now there's a community in the middle of the bush, that just get high on weed, mushrooms and space cakes. The day we decided to go to Nimbin was the Mardi Grass, and the hippies got completely naked, painted their bodies and rode round on bikes, I've never been so spun out in my life. After a few joints and special cookies the bus drove to a place where we all had a BBQ and could jump into natural pools formed by the waterfalls, had a sweet day. Now just chilling in the room, listening to Coldplay while everyone sleeps, lightweights.

Shapnin little book, missed your little black face, with Van stickers for spots. So we have been in Byron now for over a week and I've got myself a little job, I'm cleaning fucking toilets. It's not that bad because it's only for 3 hours a day and it gets me free accommodation in a sweet new hostel Nomadz. So Me and Matty are in separate hostels, it's all good, because its literally round the corner, I'm loving this new hostel, it's got a bigger kitchen, TV room and a bigger rooftop with 2 Jacuzzi's. I'm staying in an 8 bedded dorm with the rest of the staff, 2 of the girls are some Norwegian chicks we met in Bondi, Matty shagged 1 of them. Come to think of it, I don't know a girl Matty aint shagged. He is on form, girls out here love the surfer look, he doesn't even open his mouth and he has got a chick on the end of his bell end, the little rascal. We bumped into German Eddie last night, so him Felix and Matty have taken a trip to the gold coast in there van, to watch a surf comp, some of the world's best surfers are there. It's ok, I don't want to go, I mean I like cleaning poxy, filthy, rotten toilets, FML. I'm meeting some Swedish girl in the Jacuzzi in a minute, so I will see ya soon.

Hello again, been in Byron a couple of weeks now, Matty has got himself a job at the same hostel as me, so we are re-united once again. Had a nice couple of days, 1 of which we drove to a quarry to do some cliff jumping, not the best idea when my collar bone is nearly back to normal, but what an awesome adrenaline buzz. Yesterday after work I done a beach and coastal walk to the lighthouse with about 30 people from the hostel to watch the sunset, amazing views. I see my first wallaby last week when I done my morning run, and now every time I go running I end up seeing 1, they look like baby kangaroos.

Hey, Hey, Hey, been in Byron nearly a month, pretty messed up month, not gonna lie. Nomad'z hostel is mental mainly because all the staff get fucked together then go out, and because we all work at Nomadz we all get free entry everywhere and workers prices on drinks. Our room has Me, Matty Danish Daisy, Swedish Dan, Swiss Corey, Eline and Kaia from Norway and Hayley from England who I have grown very fond of. The girls do the housekeeping and find so much booze every day, so getting drunk in room 201 is pretty much free. The wildlife in Byron is so cool, I've seen Dolphins, Wallaby's, Bandicoots, Fruit Bats, Parrots, shit loads of Bush Turkeys and all sorts of colourful birds. The guys from our old hostel always come to Nomadz, because basically wherever me and Matty are is where the party starts. Me and Matty are the bollox at civil war, which is a drinking game played on the ping pong table, it's hard to walk away from that game soba. Last night we played ultimate beer pong (flip cup), it was everyone from level 1, v's level 2, and level 2 which involved room 201, smashed it. We all won more free goon. Every Friday which is today, a bunch of Christians put on huge BBQ whilst they preach, mmmmmmmm free food. To be honest Mr. Book, if you meet any tramps on your travels tell them to get there ass to Byron, because everything is free, so fucking sweet.

Hey booky! It's me Matty man. So what the hell have I been doing ay! First I have to say this place is fucking awesome, for it's like its own little world, you can't really explain it. Like the other day I dropped my shopping and this cute old lady offered me her suitcase to put my shopping in to get me home, who does that ay! 1 ultimate goal of mine has been ticked off the list in Byron, not only did I see 10x world champion Kelly Slater, but I also got the chance to speak to him, shake his hand, and surf the same waves as him. That doesn't happen every day. I've had about 12 days off from the surf at the mo, because me ribs are fucked, but there on the mend, can't wait to surf again. I've taken up skim boarding in its place, which is fucking awesome. Right I need to go everyone is playing beer pong for John's birthday and I want in so I will be back in the morning, filling the gaps from the past. I've got loads more shit to add, so black book, keep Oscar out for a couple of days. Hey booky wooky John's birthday was fucking awesome. Started drinking at 6, then we all went to Chunky Monkeys for a meal and more drinks, it was so good, because as I walked in and spoke to the reception girl for a bit and she gave me 20 drink tokens which was sweet as your only supposed to get 1. So naturally me and Tom got even more 'Dogs#!t'. Oh yeh Tom also got himself a little GET prize, for throwing a god dam stuffed monkey through a hole, it was so funny watching Tommy go mad when he won. After that everyone went back to Nomadz for more drinks, but I wanted to stay because I still had loads more drink vouchers. So I stayed there on my jacks, and entered a sex position competition, with this Canadian girl I got talking to, she was so fucking funny to do it with. We came second on the account that I kept banging away for too long in between positions, what an idiot, so no prize for Matty. A couple of hours later everyone came back to Chunky's, and was re-united once again, it went from 7pm till 3am, in Chunky's that's called a marathon, and it's a good thing if you do it, lol, 1 of my best nights because everyone was pants down 'Dogs#!t, and having a blast, what more can you ask for on a Monday.

Oi oi Mr. Bible of memories, finally Matty put pen to paper the lazy little GET. I'm loving both my jobs I'm not Tommy toilet or Hawkins housekeeping anymore, I'm Tom the trash man. I'm first in every room to wake everyone up dressed in my trash man outfit. I'm always finding money, weed, booze and little treats (weed cookies). I'm also maintenance guy for another hostel, I'm actually running out of things to do, so I have friends over there who are going to break some fences and put more holes in walls for me, happy days. Me and Matty are becoming pretty good at volleyball, our hostel take all the staff and whatever tourists want to come down to the beach and play Skim Boarding, Frisbee, Football and Volleyball. Last night was funny, me and some girl (team awesome), and Matty and some other chick (team legendary), played skateboard races down the corridor at 4am, so funny. We should stop doing these silly things, because Me, Matty, Joey, and Rhys played wheelbarrow races the other night and Joey fell on his face, and he wears glasses, funny but messed up. Its Hayley's birthday today so we are dressing up as people from the 80s tonight and doing a bar crawl. Ah Mr. book of past times, started skyping home and miss my Hawkins family so much, love them all, that's the only bad thing about travelling, missing family and friends. Life is so short Mr. Book, you really need to dream as though you will live forever, and live as though you will die today. And as the great Colonel Sanders said "I'm too drunk to taste this chicken", and as drunken Hayley says "be drunken, always. That is the point, nothing else matters. Drunken with what? With wine, with poetry or with virtue, as you please, but be drunken.

Just came in for a drink and realised fuck I love my life. Vodka and Solo says suck balls England. Matty and Tommy.

Well well well hello you little book of GETS. Although the weather is shit Byron is starting to get a lot busier because of a blues festival just round the corner coming up on the same weekend as Easter. So once it's over Me, Matty and a few others are heading north into Queensland, word on the street is that's where the suns been hiding. Had a couple of good nights out this weekend, Hayley's birthday was a good laugh. Once everyone got back to the hostel, we had a fight in room 201, girls and guys going crazy with slaps and pillows. We all need to calm down abit, because we keep getting warnings. Like when a few nights ago Me and Rhys got back to the hostel with two Swedish chicks Isabell and Makala, went into room 112 to smoke the Shabong (didgeridoo bong), and got kicked out for being too loud. Then got back to room 201, re-united with Matty and the Canadian girls, and made even more noise over more goon and weed, I don't think the night staff like us very much, ha-ha suckers. Just got back from a walk through the rainforest, with Swedish Anna, Isabell and Makala, not going to lie I shit my pants. We were deep in the forest and as we were busy keeping an eye open for Snakes and Spiders, forgot about the leaches. Fuck me Mr. Book, with your neatly drawn lines in, once Makala screamed we all ran as fast as we could for the sound of the waves, to be honest we were lost, and our only hope was the beach. As we got out and checked each other for blood sucking demons, me and Anna were fine but the others were being eaten alive, scary but fun. Now back in the room and Matty's fucked, he has been playing goon hour with the 112 crew, so I need to get involved.

Shapnin bruvva, not gonna lie my little book of crazy past times, this was the most fucked up Easter weekend ever. On Good Friday everyone from the hostel jumped in a coach to a house party a few miles from Byron, messed up night. On Saturday we all went to a market that had live music playing, after a load of goon and weed we got back to the hostel to play drinking games. I don't know why I suggested spin the bottle, but it got me in a lot of shit. I had to ride a bike naked around Byron, play the drums on pots and pans naked in the kitchen in front of my boss, shit got weird that afternoon. That night I was first home again safe and sound in bed, until Kaia and Hayley come home and literally raped me and beat me with a goon sack. It's ok though because they said surprise, so it wasn't rape, just surprise sex. Easter Sunday was a long chilled out day for me, Matty on the other hand got given a ticket to the blues fest the lucky little GET. I will let him tell you about the festival, as he tried telling me last night but couldn't talk properly. Last night was weird, 1 minute I'm teeth brushed in bed, the next I'm in the back of a campervan getting 'Dogs#!t' with 2 Swedish birds and some random English dude.

Oh my days yesterday was the most craziest shit I've done (in a while), it started with a regular day of housekeeping, with talk going round about sneaking into the last day of the festival. At the end of our shifts me, Matty, Eline and Matilda decided to try and volunteer at the Bluesfest, because Hayley and Kat phoned and told us they got in this way. So as you do in situations like this, grab your goon, weed, and welly's, and try and blag to the festival organisers to pick up rubbish and help out, when really your just going to get rat assed. As we walked in they said they had spaces for us, but because we looked abit tipsy, they told us to go walk it off for an hour, which basically meant you aint coming in. So we all walked into a fucking jungle, I shit you not Mr. Bible of Karma Sutral words, it was nuts. We climbed through barbed wire and over a river, only to realise the sun was going down and we were blatantly lost, couldn't even hear the music from the festival anymore. So once Matilda and Eline both fell into bush holes big enough you could only see their hands and feet (which has got to be the funniest thing I've ever seen) We decided to go back the way we came before Matilda's phone went dead, as it was our only torch. And I fucking hate spiders and I know they were watching me. When we finally got out, we finished off the rest of the goon, and had a joint, then went back to the front gates to try something different. Luckily Matilda got a wristband off someone leaving the festival, so as she was sending it out from inside, we managed to buy a couple of wristbands from an old couple for 40 bucks as they were leaving. As this was happening Matilda's wristband had arrived and the rest of us got in . . . . Past the first gate, but little did we know there were 2 gates and at this point we had 3 wristbands and 4 people. Unfortunately Matilda, bless her, had to leave as she was the only 1 without a wristband. Not giving up hope, as we have been through some weird shit to get this far, we planned to send 1 of our wristbands back out, when all of a sudden Matilda has come running in the festival, because she bullshitted the front desk that her wristband got stolen. It was one of the most euphoric moments of my life, when all four of us were re-united inside the bluesfest, in mud up to our knees. We got to see Elvis Costello, Bob Dylan and Grace Jones. It was an interesting experience, because it's the first time I've been to a festival full of old people, but nevertheless luck striked again, as we met some dudes who worked behind the bar and had a shit load of free beer tokens. Great Night.

Oi oi it's nice to see ya, it's always a pleasure talking to you Mr. book, its game over for Noah and Oscars Byron Bay madness. We have been here over 9 weeks and could easily stay another couple of months, but we have to do some farming if we want our second year's visa. Our last week here has been mental because the Nomads family have all decided to leave roughly at the same time, so there's a leaving do every night, gonna miss all the crazy mudda fuckers we have met here. It's a funny situation we are in at the mo, we have no money, no farm work set up, and no way of getting to anywhere, so in two days we are pretty much on our asses. We are going to try and hitchhike somewhere north. Backpacking can be scary sometimes, but that's what this is all about looking back in a few year's time and laughing at the fact that we travelled to the opposite side of the world to become homeless. Experiences like these, I believe makes you a stronger person and helps you appreciate the little things in life.

Fuck me dead, someone up there is looking after us in our times of need because we found some work picking pumpkins on our last day in Byron. After a crazy last night in Byron, me, Matty and Jordan jumped on a bus to Brisbane, because that's where the farmer was picking us up from. The send off we got from our family in Byron was very emotional, gonna miss em all so much. We arrived in Brisbane and went straight to Base Hostel as we have some free night's stay from Matty's wet-t-shirt comp in Melbourne. So as you do to meet your new roommates, get a box of goon and play some drinking games. Knowing we had to be up early to meet our farmer, me and Jordan were in bed before midnight. Matty on the other hand stayed out late busking. We had to get out of the room quick time in the morning because Matty puked in the room. So after a 5 hour journey into the bush we arrived at Yelarbon. It's a town with a population of about 30 people. Now little Mr. Bible of dreams, before we left Byron we all said at our new place we wanted to detox and get fit. So as we arrived in this town with a dozen houses, a store with fuck all in it and a hotel with a pub. Guess where we are staying, yes in the fucking pub. Oh well the detox plan was a nice thought for a while. So the first night here, we met our new family member Stefan (some English dude from the west country). It's us 4 who are going to clear this farm of pumpkins. Matty and Jordan had a movie night in our new pad, which is the sickest place yet. It's like a two bedroom massive caravan, TV and DVD, huge kitchen and a garden between us and the pub with a trampoline, pool and 3 dogs (mum and 2 pups). So me and Stefan got 'Dogs#!t' in the pub and ended up at a bonfire with a load of incested weirdo's. This place is full of random weirdo's. Well they are all stuck in a town surrounded by farms and only 1 shit pub, so I don't blame them for being abit weird.

Mr. booky magic wooky! It's been to long since you last see my handwriting. So much has happened these last couple of weeks. I've had my bar crawl job of justice which was pretty fun, reminded me of my Kavos days. I made abit of money, so I thought why not buy some wheels for my skateboard, only to find out that I had a big fat zero in the bank, so I sold them to a kid for under half the price. Nice 1 Matty thinking on your feet again, lol. Me and Tommy have been partying harder than ever since us both and everyone else decided to leave Byron. Been skating so much on my new z-flex which I'm gonna name right now Zeek, is what he shall be named. Met this sweet dude called Pierre who owned a skateboard, he showed me some stuff which was so cool to learn, getting better every day. Gonna be dogtown soon. Gonna miss Nomads a lot, partying, eating pies, rape nights in 201, and just having a blast. This past week has been abit of a tossup for me, great and weird, mixed emotions going around, but all good just got to get my act together at times. Now Yelarbon, are we really here! Because it was only 2 days ago we were skint, had no-where to go, give our only jobs away, and had no plans. Kinda like the feeling of having nothing, because then you don't have much to worry about, but a plan is sometimes good to have. It's all down to the ginger 1, without him I defo would not be in Yelarbon, probably thumbing it somewhere. You're gonna read this Tommo and think yeh I am the man, but really you was just the only 1 with credit on your phone and a bit of patience. But seriously cooto's to you man, you have made this shit happen, I'm gonna get off my ass from now on. So after throwing up, busking with a guy with no teeth what so ever, partying and getting off with 'Dogs#!t' birds, lol, we went from Brissy to farmland. Just had our first day's work, got up at 6.30am and picked (blue) pumpkins for most of the day, before it started raining. To be honest it really wasn't that bad, might be first day thrills but it was coolio. It's kinda funny when you think about it, was only 2 days ago we was partying in Chunky Monkey's and now we are on a random farm in the middle of no-where picking pumpkins. It's funny where you go and how things work out booky boy.

Pumpkin picking is going really well actually really enjoying it, but the only problem is we are all working to fast. It's gone from a month's work to about 2 and half weeks. They all need a bit of Matty work mentality, slow and steady wins the race, lol. Our boss Carl is wicked and his mum does an excellent job being the dinner lady and chit chat provider. Bless her little cotton socks, good old Marge. Yesterday's work was the best, because we have been straight picking for 2 days nothing else, just 4 men, 1 field and over 100,000 pumpkins, which is unreal. But after all that picking we got to mess around on the truck for most of the afternoon, throwing pumpkins at each other's heads, it was hilarious, even Carl was involved. Then after a hard day's work we came home straight to the pub and got 'Dogs#!t', it was weird because I haven't drunk for a whole week so was drunk even quicker than usual if that's possible. After 40 games of pool the 4 of us were falling asleep at bonfires, throwing up, and trying to watch the end of kung fu panda, what a messy night for the boys of the Butlins lookalike caravan.

Wow I know what you're thinking Mr. Book Matty has wrote more than 3 pages, he must have been high or something. Just letting you know week 1 of pumpkin mayhem is over, followed by a crazy pissed up weekend of getting 'Dogs#!t' with the locals. Today was a good day, our boss Carl picked us up and took us to a river to go fishing. I'm actually sitting here now watching Jordan and Stefan eat the fish I caught. Me and Matty had chicken and pasta, fuck fish. It was nice all 5 of us took 2 boats and a crate of beer to find Nimo and friends. We almost capsized the boat, thank fuck Jordan was the only 1 to fall in, so funny. It's a shame this outback experience is coming to an end, I really like it here. I'm getting fit as well as slowly overcoming my fear of spiders. In Australia there are 3 species of spiders you really need to be careful of: Funnel web, White tip and Red back. Believe it or not the farm is full of White tips and Red backs, beautiful spiders to be honest, but deadly. Looking forward to next weekend, some of the locals are taking us hunting, for Kangaroos and wild pigs. There are kangaroos and Emu's everywhere, they are classed as vermin but illegal to kill. Some weird laws out here like if you come across a snake you're not allowed to kill it, just re-locate it. So we are all gonna take 2 hunting dogs and a rifle each to blow some pigs head off.

Gooday Cunt, I know it's not a nice word but the Aussie's use the "C" word as often as the English people use the word "The". Well we have said goodbye to Yelarbon, as we have picked over 100 tonnes of pumpkins in 2 weeks. We are gonna miss Carl and his family they were really good to us, with money food and even finding us more work. So after another days fishing and a Sunday roast, Carl drove us across the border to his friend's farm in NSW, for some more pumpkin picking. Stefan has gone cotton picking, thank fuck, bit of a nob head. Me, Matty and Jordan arrive at our new house, it's a 3 bedroom house on the guys farm to ourselves, it's the first time I've had my own room since England. It's not as furnished as our last pad but it's free, and not next to a pub, so we can detox properly and save some money.

Hello Mr. black book of big up ya breasts in a bag of bullshit, I can't believe I've not committed suicide, farm work is a load of bollox. We have completed our first week of picking at our new farm and only another week left, thank fuck. I'm sure if the almighty sends me to hell I will be picking pumpkins down there. We miss the beach so much and I am sure we are slowly losing the plot. The highlight of my day is looking forward to having a cup of tea and doing a crossword puzzle in the back of a porno mag, I was better off cleaning fucking toilets in Byron. Anywho, we have only 1 week left then heading as far north as possible towards the sun, sea, sand and sex. Ah god how I miss them 4 words. I think our plan is to go to Darwin via Ayres Rock, as far away from New South Wales as possible. It now makes sense why they call it NSW, because the South of Wales in Britain is full of inbred's, just like this place.

Hello again I thought I would write something as there's fuck all else to do. It's the 1st June, wow, been in Oz 5 months today, crazy shit. Last night we got some goon and climbed on the roof of our cottage to watch the stars, many of which were shooting stars. It's amazing for stars out here as we are so far away from any lit up areas. Our cottage is in the middle of a farm surrounded by hundreds of cows, it's funny walking around of a night with a torch and seeing shit loads of eyes.

Booksta, how are u? You know Tommy boy them fucking cows. I think I'm starting to conquer my fear of the darkness. It started with me walking back from the good old farmer's house with no light at all and no friends☹. Tommy and Jordan left without me, because of my number of downloads using the farmer's internet. It got to the point where they were too far ahead for me to run and catch up, so I stayed at the house and eventually braved it on my own. I walked out the front door got to the end of the drive, shitting myself, couldn't see anything. Kept walking to the light of our house in the field, then it faded and thought oh it will be alright, but then I couldn't see it again and started to get scared of the cows and roo's. But then realised it was alright because I had walked into Ted's shed no wonder I couldn't see the house. I eventually made it back on the road, found the little bridge we have to cross, then walked so fast past all the cows ducking to the floor for some reason, ha-ha. A 5 minute walk took me in the dark a good 20 minutes, scary shit, was happy to see the house with the

boys in it. Very quick story, but had to be told, ask me Matty Mat Mat for more details of this encounter.

Wot shapnin Mr. Bible of justice, so the pumpkins are over thank fuck. So as we were deciding where next, our farmer Ted offered us 6 more weeks of picking cotton, as much as we just wanna get out of here, we need the work to extend our visa, so we took on the offer and were taught how to use the module builders to press the cotton, and now are pretty god dam awesome cotton picking sons of bitches. 2 new guys have moved into our cottage to help us pick the cotton, they're alright for northern monkeys. Me and Matty every Saturday morning go down to the local school and teach them how to play football (soccer). It's so funny the kids love it so much more now me and Matty are coaching. It's the highlight of our week teaching them kids, there's fuck all else to do. We have been blessed with a DVD player, but are sick of that already. And it's now started raining, which means we can't pick cotton because it fucks the machinery being wet, and believe it or not compressed wet cotton can catch on fire. So it looks like we have 3 or 4 days off, which can only mean goon o clock.

So farming let's talk about that, 6 weeks in and me and Tommy are only bloody half way aren't we, so we have gone from pumpkins to cotton, and after driving me first tractor to my first cotton builder, things are looking up on the responsible side. We have had 4 days of watching about 10 million DVD's and still going strong because of this god dam rain. So naturally in those invigorating days on the farm resort, we got 3 cases of goon in and had ourselves a party. Stereo up, furniture everywhere and eggs up the wall from me and Tommy playing fragger in real life form, lol. The new boys Danny and Tommy went to Sydney for a few days and got 'Dogs#!t' where there were actual girls in real life form, lucky fuckers. So the rain has gone for a bit and back to work we went. Me and Jordan went to Ted's brother's farm to pick up sticks and stones for 7 hours, whilst Tommy fixed a couple of chairs and general handyman shit around Ted's house. Wasn't all bad though because Ted's brother William left us to our own devices for the day, so I drove the car all day round the farm, basically a full days driving lesson. So after sticks, *stones and a full days driving, I was about to get out the driving seat to let Jordan drive back to the house, but Will came up on the quad bike, so I put the brakes on and said hey, thought he was gonna say what the hell are you doing, but he was sweet meat. Said some shit I can't remember, then allowed me to drive back to the house and park it up. I got the car back in 1 piece and was laughing my head off, thinking he doesn't know me well enough to let me drive his car. Definitely wanna drive Aussie land on my second year, would be so fucking awesome.*

Hello Mr. book, fancy seeing you round here, well another week or so gone and can honestly say haven't got a clue what tomorrow brings. Because of the floods earlier on this year the cotton just isn't ready or just fucked completely, so this last week we have been doing all sorts. Me and Matty went to Will and Pam's farm to clear up some paddocks fucked from the floods, basically made bonfires and drove round in a Ute all day, good fun, hopefully Pam will get her tits out the little MILF. These last couple of days I've been doing some woodwork in Greg and Lisa's house, building walls, tiling bathrooms, plastering ceilings, aint got a fucking clue what I'm doing, but fuck it I need the money. The other day I spoke to my Aussie bank over the phone, and the security question they ask me to verify who I am is "what colour are your pubes?" It's fucking hilarious every time I phone them, some of the staff actually know me because of that question. Its funny because they try being professional, but can't help laughing. Mr. book could you transform into a few hundred dollars so I can fly my mum out here, I miss her so much, if you do I will treat ya to a new pen, cheers, ta.

Hey booky man, so another week has passed, getting closer now to that visa. Just had another morning of footy with the kids. This week me and Tommy swopped round, I had the bigger kids and he had the little ones. Although the bigger kids kick more of the football, there was a lack of wrestling on the pitch which I'm used to with the young lings. It well made me miss them bubble gum, flower kicking moe foes. For instance at half time all the kids except the little ones were back on the pitch ready for the second work out, while the little ones were in the sand pit making Tommy push them on the zip wire thing, was well funny. Anyways got to rush back to the cotton, that's enough fun for one morning.

Gooday there Mr. Book, it's nearly July and half way through winter, I can honestly say it's the only winter I've managed to keep a tan. I'm back on the cotton today, as Jordan has left to meet his parents on the east coast. It's been quality working at the Funlay's house, I've been driving quad bikes, Utes and cars round whilst doing my chippy work. See a wallaroo the other day, it's basically a big black kangaroo, the roads are so dangerous the fuckers are everywhere. Got to go, wanna go flirt with Ted's wife before work, see ya.

Oi Oi, shapnin Mr. bible, I'm sitting here at the moment with a pack of 6 Tooheys, outside the cottage with classic 90's tunes playing in the winter sun, which is at least 20 degrees, whilst the boys are at work, happy days. I joined Matty last week for a few days at Will and Pam's farm, driving the Ute up and down collecting sticks, so they don't get caught in the cotton picker. Had a little moment that day, as we was standing in front of the Ute which was seconds away from blowing up as we over heated the engine and the cotton in the fan caught on fire, it started raining only for a few minutes and a double rainbow came up right in front of us, the end of the rainbow was only 50 meters away. A moment me and Matty call Sagapo my life. It's an actual Sagapo my life moment right now, Tiesto, Silence, Dilerium has just come on, this will always remind me of me and my brother Russell's ally pally night in London. Only four weeks left then hopefully I can re-kindle that night on the east coast once more.

What's up booksta, well I will tell ya what's up, we have only gone and picked all the fucking cotton, thank fuck for that. It's a relief to see the back of that shit, we are only 2 weeks short of doing our 88 days, so either we will stay and do odd jobs or just fuck off as Ted said he don't mind signing us off a few weeks, to be honest could do with another couple of weeks wages, so it looks like we are staying. The next time we speak book, will be back on the coast because I know you're probably getting bored of this farming shit. See ya.

Ok not left the farm yet, but just booked our bus out of here and thought you should know, so excited. It was our last day of soccer training today with the kids, gonna miss them little fuckers, especially the Beugle crew. Me and Matty babysitted all 7 Beugle kids the other week and they are hard work but fun to be around. Next weekend we have got an all weekend piss up at the Texas show, which is gonna be a great send of for us, as everyone in town will be there.

The Texas show was jokes, I felt like a celebrity, everyone knew us and we got given V.I.P treatment, free food and drink in the V.I.P box, happy days. We went on loads of rides with the kids and entered in a competition, me and Matty were in a team with three others called the misfits, our team come last, I lost a rock wall climb, Mat lost on the greasy donkey and apart from one victory on the tug of war, and we lost that as well. So after the competition and the fireworks, we got 'Dogs#!t', great day.

Waaaaaaaaaaaaaa and Matty says Wooooooooooooooooo, we are here, ok its only Brisbane which is like a shit version of Melbourne, but no more cotton, pumpkins, tractors, cow shit or a cottage with a few lads like a scene from Brokeback mountain, farming is done. Today we walked round the city and went shopping for some new little GETS and got $1000 of tax back, I've now got the money to back up my new hair style.

Well said millionaire Tommy, it feels so good being off that god dam farm. So as we walked round brissy today, we were surrounded by so many GETS. My GET radar is back on. Brissy is alright but a bit boring, just think it's like that because of the no beach situation. Me and Tom celebrated today by getting a Boost and some nice little treats, been too long in farm clothes not to.

First night on the piss last night, ended up in me throwing up in the smoking area in our hostel, and Tom eating more than his body weight in kebabs. Let's hope for more 'Dogs#!tness' tonight. Yeeeeewwwwww.

Booky so the heartache of Brisbane is over thank fuck. No more city know it all's for a while. So we took the plane from Brissy to Cairns. I've got to say so far what a place. Reminds me of pictures of California. Checked into Nomadz with intentions of scoring a job there, (success by the way). Got into the room at 1am, took one look at the beds and thought fuck this, when life gives you lemons, bail. So we did, got 'Dogs#!t' to the max in a couple of hours, and looked at so many GETS it was a joke. Next day was sweet as, took a look round Cairns, got some more new shit. Then just chilled on the grass catching the last of the suns ever gazing rays. Met some cool people in the room so gonna get wasted with them and try and win some more free shit, wish me luck.

We are settled in and have landed right on our feet. Love Cairns, this town is not massive, has just the right amount of shops, pubs and clubs. There is an artificial beach in town, a bit like the one in Brisbane, because they don't want people sitting on the beaches here as it would be like a buffet for crocs. Me and Matty are doing housekeeping with some other French chick Lulu. Its fucking sweet we do about half hours work, then sit in our room and watch a film till the end of our shift, this gets us free accommodation and a free dinner, we are loving up all the free shit. Just yesterday we entered in a free scuba diving lesson, which involved a running race under water in our scuba shit. Matty won the race and got us a 2-for-1 scuba dive on the Great Barrier Reef, something that was going to cost us $300 is now $125. We played poker last night trying to win a 2-for-1 skydive, but no luck, so we are going to wait to win one until we book it. Every night our hostel do competitions in the bar to win these prizes so hopefully it won't be long.

Vud doin, you little GET, been in Cairns now a few weeks, not gonna lie shits getting weird. We have re-united with Anna, Matilda, Kaia, Eline, Hayley and M, we all used to work in Byron Bay together. We also have a new member to the "let's get Dogs#!t crew", Jewbag. He arrived last week and loving it already. Yesterday was a goodun, after housekeeping, me, Matty, Lewis (Jewbag) and three French people drove to the rainforest and chilled out by the waterfalls all day, another Sagapo my life moment. Last night I got up on the bar in "Penutbutter-o Brian's" and entered a pole dancing competition, I came second, gutted, I should have won. Matty entered it last week and also came second, I got us a couple of free pints though, which was sweet. Cairns festival is on at the moment, there's outdoor cinema screens, carnivals and all kinds of free shit, happy days. We have got shit load of excursions coming up, so this next week is gonna be sweet.

Dear diary, I fucking love my life, a few days this week we drove to the mountains and went trekking through rainforests, we went to a place called crystal cascades, the waterfalls there were very nice, but we took a path to a hidden waterfall and it was amazing we were the only four people there. As we were sitting on the rocks we found a pipe with a tin of weed, proper random, I think it was a message from god saying if there was ever a time to smoke weed it's now. The crystal clear pools at the bottom of the waterfalls were freezing cold, but so sweet. We see turtles swimming around which I was really pleased about because we went scuba diving the other day and didn't see any turtles. That day was fucking awesome, the boat that took us to the Great Barrier Reef did not stop feeding us all day. Scuba diving is one of the best things I've ever done, it's another world down there, I cannot explain how beautiful, (Tommy fell asleep, Matty finishes) *all the shit is down there, it's like stepping into Finding Nemo or Sharks Tail. So ok I really really love my god dam life right now. Meeting all the girls from Bondi and Byron, doing so much daytime stuff, yeeehhh. The night time has been so sick as well, but where ever we go people are not astonished that we go out every bloody night, getting asked if we are alcoholics must be a sign. The 'Dogs#!t' levels must be raised instantly, but seriously trying to stay in a bit more as we don't want to just throw all the farming money away at the bar. All this stuff that is happening right now is just flipping amazing, can't believe it's still going sometimes. So just GET. You can't GET if you aint got that GET.*

Wooooo just been fucking skydiving, it was the best thing I've ever done, and its definitely not the last one I'm doing, if I had the money I would love to become an instructor. We jumped at 40,000 feet, it was a free fall for 60 seconds, and then 10,000 feet later the parachute opens. I cannot explain the feeling, it's better than any rave, party, drug or orgy I've ever been in or done. We are leaving Cairns tonight and heading 5 hours south to Magnetic Island, where a full moon party awaits. September 2011 is probably going to be the best month of my life, thank you dirty rotten pumpkins and filthy itchy cotton, you made this happen.

On the bus what a night and day, words cannot explain the shiz nizz right now, can't see shit because of the no light business on the bus and the fact that me Lew and Tom smoked a mumma of a joint. I mean I don't know what to do with my hands. Skydive, everything, all of this, things could not be better. Here we go on the busy bus bus.

Wow I was expecting Magnetic Island to be a run-down touristy shit hole because of the full moon partys, but it's one of the most beautiful places in Oz I've ever seen. We got here Tuesday morning and the full moon party isn't until Friday, so we have decided to not drink and explore this island until Friday. Yesterday we rented out some bicycles and took a ride round the island, it was fucking hard work, it seemed every road was up hill and was so fucking hot, but it was well worth it. We visited many bays with beaches, our first bay had shit load of rock wallaby's, we sat down and fed them coconut as there are coconut trees everywhere on this island, we then sat there and looked out to sea. There's so much coral reef surrounding this island and because of this we got to see some really cool fish and a turtle the size of a coffee table, with a baby turtle on its back. Lewis who is determined to catch a fish, got out his travel fishing wire and hook with a bit of coconut for bait and caught a fish within 30 seconds, unfortunately couldn't keep the fish as it's illegal to keep the catch here, awesome start to the day. We then road to a walking path, parked up our bikes and trekked up a mountain to see some amazing views and a koala bear only arm's length away chilling in the trees. There so cute but riddled with chlamydia so would rather stay at arm's length.

I'm laying here now in my hammock looking forward to a chilled out day, as tomorrow's full moon party is going to be messy. com. After writing in this diary, the boys were still not up so I took a walk to a secret nude beach, which me and Lewis found a few days ago, but obviously didn't want to go together. So I trekked down the side of this mountain to find a rock spray painted with the words "nudes only", so I got naked and had the whole beach to myself, it was perfect. I went naked swimming, naked rock climbing, and a sneaky naked fag, it was perfect.

Well fuck me dead, the full moon party was wicked, roughly 1500 people turnt up to party in our hostel, our room was the one closest to the bar, there were people dancing outside our door till six in the morning. During the day one of the organisers offered us free drink if we help set up the event (move tables and other random shit), it was hard work but well worth it, because it got us six drinks each free that night, which went down a treat. It was an awesome night, don't get me wrong it was a shabby attempt to try and re-enact the Thailand full moon party, but still a total success of meeting the most random people, whilst raising the 'let's get Dogs#!t' levels to the max. The next day we heard an announcement that the after party starts at 10am, so after a couple of hour's sleep we crawled to the bar and had jugs of snake bite and shots of Jagerbombs for breakfast. All the staff, djs, us and few other randoms still going strong from the night before, got smashed all day and night. We had a game of slip and slide set up during our day of carnage. It was a big tarpaulin, hosed down with washing up liquid, it was such a laugh until one of the meatheads thought it would be funny to jump in head first whilst someone was already sliding the other way, and split his head open. Apart from that mishap it was an awesome weekend. On Sunday we jumped on our five hour bus journey to Airlie beach, which so far I can say is amazing, beautiful scenery and wicked nightlife, only been one day though so let's see how it goes.

We are now on day three on Airlie Beach, and shits getting weird. When you travel in Oz through hostels, you make friends and create little families. The family we met on Maggy Island are travelling down the coast roughly the same time we are, so we have been getting on it in a big group. Last night I was first home again, but this time was a wise decision because on the way home Mat and Lewis got in a fight and Lewis got arrested for having a knife on him, he thinks he is Bear Grylls crossed with Crocodile Dundee. Tonight we are chilling out, because we are sailing round the Whit Sunday Islands on what we keep getting told by everyone is a sex party boat, happy days.

Well suck me sideways, the Atlantic Clipper sail boat is fucking god dam finger licking good. We set sail around 3pm heading to the Whit Sundays. Unfortunately the ratio from men to women was poor and not in our favour but we were allowed to take our own booze on board so it wasn't the end of the world. We got to our first island and dropped the anchor in time for dinner at sunset. After dinner the drinking games began, it was a pukka first night, we met some wicked people, especially Steve the pirate who's name wasn't Steve. The crew on board were so fucked up, they made us get into groups and act out different scenes as different characters. Our group smashed it, we had a French guy who couldn't really talk English playing Michael Jackson, Matty as an Australian, I was an Essex girl which I've got down to a tee and Steve the pirate as a Sail Boat Skipper. We had to be in our cabins at midnight as we had to be up for breakfast at 6.30am.

After breakfast we sailed to the most beautiful beach in the world, Whitehaven Beach. The white sands on the beach are the finest sands in the world, in fact if you use it to clean your teeth, they go two shades whiter. As we went for a little swim in our stinger suits, we got to see massive sting rays, scary but sweet. After the beach we got back to the boat, which was anchored in the middle of a turtle breeding ground. One of the turtles we see was at least two meters round. We wasn't allowed to go swimming or snorkeling here, as it was full of tiger sharks, I mean I know turtles are cool but fuck getting eaten just to get close to one. We set sail to our next spot to do some snorkeling, as well as using the diving board and slide on our boat, which was in the middle of so much beautiful reef, so loads of fish to see. After we had lunch we sailed to our next spot, where we anchored for the night. On the way a few eagles were lingering above, when the skipper pulled out a pack of sausages and started to feed the eagles during mid-flight. It was awesome Eddie the eagle and his mate Bob, swooped down to catch there munch, fucking love this boat. After we anchored and had dinner, which by the way was some good shit, we sat on the top deck watching sharks swimming around the boat, as well as some of the brightest stars I've seen, another Sagapo my life moment. We then endured another messed up night of drinking games involving dressing up and getting naked, it was wicked, bearing in mind there were more sausages flying around more than what we see the eagles eat, the handful of girls did get there Bristol's out, which was sweet. After crawling into bed about 1.30am we had to be up for breakfast at 6.30am. Absolute killer, but it is what we paid for so fuck it.

We spent a few hours snorkeling around cook island, which was named after James Cook who discovered Australia in 1770, who then told his majesty not to do the obvious thing and move the British here for good, but send all the fucking criminals here to the most beautiful country in the world, who then have the power a few hundred years later, to have the cheek to make me pick pumpkins just to see it, Rant Over. Anyway after spending the morning at James the Nobheads Island we sailed back to Airlie Beach. On the way back, we see a shit load of whales, it was a great end to a great trip. Now just getting ready to go out, it's Saturday night and everyone from the boat is meeting up to get 'Dogs#!t' again.

Well look who it is, I'm all good booky wooky thanks for asking. So we are in 1770, and loving it here. Wasn't enjoying the 10 hour tight as arsholes bus journey though, but getting baked before we got on the bus, made it a bit funnier. So 1770 is a really nice town, and the hostel we are staying in is possibly the best hostel we have stayed in yet. The biggest chill out place in the world, there's tonnes of hammocks lying around, lovely little pad in the jungle, etc. The woman here who owns it is like this old timer hippy, she's so nice. First night here we treated ourselves to a massive BBQ on the Barbie, it was wicked. Had some nice chicken hearts that's give me some unbelievable poo. After all that just chilled out in the room for a bit, then headed down to the camp fire. Met this cool Aussie who was rubber tramping it around Oz in his van. He was telling us some pretty unreal stories, so now if we do a road trip, gonna make sure we are over prepared, don't wanna get bummed by the hills have eyes folk . . . . really I don't. So me, Tom and Lew, oh yeah and the Aussie guy, were sitting around this fire, guitars, weed, beers and a killer shooting star. We woke up to toast, marmalade and coffee, then to the beach to hit some long awaited waves. Yes booky that's what I thought, suck my tanned salted nut sacks England.

Welcome back Mr. Bitch ass book, with ya black square face. The three day tour on Fraser Island, was the best three days of my life. We checked into a hostel on rainbow beach, dumped our bags in the room and went for a wonder. I love Rainbow beach, it reminds me of Byron Bay in a way. The beach is a never-ending, immaculate piece of art with some sweet surf. The surrounding town is very small and hippyfied, full of some of the happiest people. There are also some massive sand dunes, which Me, Matty, Lewis, Dave, Chekas and Charlotte all went to for some sand boarding, some boomerang practice and a beautiful sunset. It's really random, Dave, Chekas and Charlotte met us in Maggy Island, since then we have bumped into them every stop on the way down, it's a shame we are not on the same tour as them on Fraser Island.

The next day we woke up to meet our tour guide Monkey, who made this trip the best it could be, along with our new 15 friends we are going to be camping with. We had two 4x4 jeeps, Monkey, Me, Mat, Lewis, couple from Denmark, an Irish and an English girl in one car, and three guys and five girls in the other jeep. We packed up all our camping equipment, food and booze, and jumped on a ferry from Rainbow Beach to Fraser Island. There are no roads on this island, which is the biggest sand island in the world. After a good sing along driving down this never-ending beach, we set up camp to have lunch. Then we drove inland up and down these awesome sand tracks to the most amazing lake I've ever seen, Lake Mckensie. The sands on this island are just as white and fine as they were on the Whit Sunday Islands and the water on this lake was so clear it looked fake. Once we all had a swim, we drove to a walking track through a rainforest and tasted water from a natural creek, purer than anything I've tasted. This island sits on a massive water pocket, created from the last ice age, so constantly the creeks, lakes and springs have pure clean water running through them, roughly a few million gallons an hour. There are places on this island not safe to drive as huge water/sand pockets can swallow jeeps whole (sinking sand). As we were driving back to camp, we got in a bit of a traffic jam, because of a jeep in front getting bogged in deep sand. So all of us jumped out and managed to get them out, ahhh bless our little family all sticking together, Monkey and his mad mission crew don't fuck about. We then drove to find a spot to plot up a camp on the beach. It was like something out of the TV show shipwrecked, all of us working together to help set up our tents and the kitchen area. After all the girls cooked a lovely stir fry for everyone, the drinking games started. I ended up spending the night on the beach with some Austrian bird getting up to all sorts, under the most amazing night sky. Normally backpacker's sex has just been meaningless, short and shit, but that night . . . . that night was different.

Next morning after breakfast we had a swim down a creek for a shower and hangover cure. Then drove along a beach to a lookout point called Indian Heads, the views from up here were spectacular. We see Sharks, Whales and Manta Rays bigger than cars. We then took a rock climb to a place called champagne pools, a little disappointed because there was no champagne, but did get to see a massive jellyfish. We then drove through more beaches and inland tracks to a place where we had lunch, then climbed up sand dunes to Frasers highest point, more amazing views, again Sagapo my god dam life. We then drove to a lake filled with natural tea tree oil, it's weird, not had a shower since we left rainbow beach, but feel the cleanest I've ever felt. This lake was also filled with loads of fresh water turtles, who loved to nibble your toes. We also see a massive water spider, freaky but in some ways beautiful. We all then drove back to the camp for a spag bol cooked by the boys, followed by another hard core drinking session. This night the sky was even clearer and you could see the Milky Way perfectly.

At 4.30 in the morning we all got up and trekked to the sand dunes to watch the sun rise, fucking early but well worth it. Then had a nice day of chilling out before packing up camp. These last few days we have been singing along to the artist Ed Sheeren and on the way back to the ferry we come across a shipwreck and wrote all our names on it with a few quotes of Eddy Sheeren. As we was in the queue for the ferry we see a few dolphins right up close to shore. Once on the ferry we see loads of jellyfish passing through the passage which splits up Rainbow Beach and Fraser Island. As I looked back on the island at all the wild dingo's running up and down the beaches, I thought to myself, if there's one place on earth I've been the happiest ever (apart from West Ham getting promoted back to the Premiership) it was this island. Monkey took us all on one last swim, when we got back to mainland, which was a bit scary after seeing in the last three days at least five species of marine life that can kill in these same waters, but still a great end to a great trip.

So the book of good and great times, how the hell are you. So came back from Fraser and checked into our hostel, with everyone from the trip. Was well funny all the boys in one room and all the girls in the room next door. We all planned to get fucked up that night with all the goon we had left over, but it turns out that the Fraser Monkey Missions hit us a lot harder than we thought. We decided to take a nap and all woke up the next morning like what the fuck is the time. Sadly all the guys left that day and only me Tommy and Lewis was left, but was wicked because Mr. monkey man turned up and offered to take us paddle boarding, we was all syked for it. First time ever on one of those boards and it was a wicked experience. Me and Lewis fell in a bunch of times, but Tom held strong and didn't fall in once. But after being told there were bull sharks in there I'm not surprise he wasn't first in for play time. We then went back to Monkeys sweet pad and had dinner. His friend went fishing and caught a 20k Tuna, so we all put five bucks in for sides and had the biggest feast ever. But wait there's more. Chilling after the big meal, Monkey pops up with a bag of weed and says game on. We were so baked, bongs flying about everywhere, I've never eaten so many lolly pops in my life. When we finally got back to the hostel, new people were in our room. Was so funny trying to keep conversations with them, without our minds drifting with the birdies. But they were cool, one girl even made me a peanut butter sandwich, cheers ta.

Next day was an early start, was out the door by 7 o clock to take another paddle with Monkey again, and was so peaceful that time in the morning. Paddling through all the jungle was fucking sweet, finally we had to say by to the Monkey man, was sad because he totally changed the outlook on a lot of things in life in general, what you go through, what it throws at you and how you deal with it. Gonna miss that big chimp, he made Rainbow and Fraser for us guys. Definatly one of the best guys ive ever met, so thank you Monkey man. Another Greyhound Bus later we hit our latest destination, Noosa baby. We was only there two nights, but was a really nice place to see, very chilled out. We stayed in a flashpackers hostel. I know what you're thinking Me and Tom in a flashpackers you must be kidding. But for what it had there, was cheap as. Wi-Fi, surfboards, two pillows, sweet bed and a killer shower. The best shower ever, I want one of those bad boys one day. The waves weren't bad down there, so we all went for a surf. Was one of my best surfs I've had. Not much to say about the night, just kicked back and had a BBQ and watched a few films, because I haven't seen one in a while.

Oh my little book, a sad time has come Noah and Oscar have had to split. We left Noosa to arrive to some random place on the sunshine coast, because all three of us had a job interview there. After walking around this town looking for a hostel, we decided fuck the job let's get out of this shithole. Now because I had another interview set up in Brisbane two days later. I booked my bus there, however Matty booked his bus to Byron Bay. Jealous as me and Lewis was to watch Matty continue to Byron, good luck was afoot, because I nailed the interview and start next week, it's the first ever office job I've had. Lewis kinda has no choice but to stay in or around Brisbane because his court case is coming up, also my little brother Scott arrives here next week, so I'm glad we are here to meet him. Today Me and Lewis had a day's work cleaning someone's house up for a bit of cash. Lovely people, after we finished we stayed and watched the AFL final, it's basically an Australian retarded game of rugby, but was the final so was fun to watch.

Ah we meet again my bible of justice, we have been in Brisbane over a week now and yes believe it or not it has been messy.com. After working the weekend painting and cleaning and nearly breaking all my fingers, I started my weeks training at my new job, it was wicked. Met some awesome people and learned a lot about sales in training. We have been doing some fun team building exercises and go pub after work, think I'm gonna like this job. Geek boy (Scott) arrived last week he has settled in and enjoying Oz. He and Lew are going to work on a farm in a few days, so I'm going to be alone in Brisbane. If this job goes tits up I'm going to meet them on the farm, hopefully it goes well and I make loads of sales. Mad weekend we just had, I woke up Saturday morning and booked us all a bus to Byron Bay, we only went for the night and got the bus back Sunday afternoon. It was so good to see Matty and my old pals, really didn't want to leave, Byron is my second home. It was a messy night.

Where the fuck ave you been, it's been 2-3 weeks since we last spoke, I managed to stick out my sales job for a few weeks, but sold fuck all, so I quit one Thursday afternoon. That night I spoke to Greg Funlay, the farmer who's house I was building a few months back and he said he will have some work for me starting next week. So Friday morning I grabbed my toothbrush and a spare pair of pants and jumped on a train to Surfers Paradise on the Gold coast. It was wicked a few friends I met up the coast were there (Dave and Chekas), it was chekas b-day Friday night so it was an awesome surprise for her. I met so many cool people, the guys stay in a room with 16 people and everyone in the room was a mess head, the whole weekend was crazy. I absolutely love them lot I met, I hope I see them again. The hostel had a swimming pool with a volleyball net, so we all got gooned up and played boy's v's girls. I was with the girls because the girls had the shallow end and I couldn't stand up in the deep end, and we kicked ass. We all went out again that night, which was wicked.

Surfers is a great place to go out, I'm definitely coming back here. The Sunday night I got back to Brisbane, I got back to my room and all my stuff was still there thank fuck. I met some Norwegian chick who I pulled the week before by saying in Norwegian, "do u shag as well as you dance", we went down into the bar under our hostel. We wasn't there for long until we got back to our hostel and has sex in the lift, on the balcony, in the corridor and in the showers. Great end to a great weekend. So Monday I got picked up by a truck driver in Brissy, who give me a lift to Texas, fuck me what the hell am I doing back here. Scott and Lewis were working on another farm when I arrived, but now we are re-united and working together on Greg's farm, getting all the paddocks ready for planting for the cotton and peanut harvest. It's us three and two Swedish blokes living in Greg and Lisa's house.

This time round my farming experience has been so much better than my first. My first week I was driving a tractor 13 hours a day right through till early hours in the morning. My tractor had a GPS, so I basically sat on my ass listening to shabby Aussie radio and truck drivers having arguments on the two way radio. Australian wildlife comes to life at night, kangaroos, emu's, snakes, the lot, wicked experience. We all have a quad bike each to get to and from the farms, and they are so much fun especially when it rains. So far I've crashed my tractor into a pivot and Scott has broken his tractor for not checking the petrol, twice. We finished work early today so we borrowed Greg's paddle board and went down the river, four people on one board is hard work especially when your stonned. I'm keeping in touch with Matty who makes me jealous every time I speak to him, living it up in Byron, miss that little GET. Unfortunately for me I'm skint and need to save for Thailand, which is only a month away, and I know deep down if I go Byron to stay, I won't save a penny and probably won't leave.

Big Fat 'smoo' to you Mr. Bible, what a pukka week we have had. Me, Scott and the two Swedish dudes took a road trip to

Byron Bay, Lewis stayed on the farm, don't ask why! After a four hour journey down the windiest road known to man, a good drink and many piss breaks we arrived in Byron. Me and Scott checked into Nomads, while Nick and Fred stayed in another hostel with their friends from home. We met up with Matty and the crew and carried on getting on it. Ready for Mexican Monday Madness. In Chunky Monkey's that night I bumped into an old friend, a Scottish girl I met in Kavos in 2006, wee Gem. The next morning me and Scott bought some legal weed and went to the beach for a smoke. When we got back to the hostel, everyone was drinking, so after a bottle of vodka and a box of goon, we had a big game of goon pong with the Nomadz crew and the Swedish boys. Unfortunately I didn't make it out late that night, as I got chucked out of Woopy's bar for falling asleep in the smoking area, Scott managed to get me back to the hostel and as we were having a fag outside some German girl offered us a threesome, as fucked as I was left Scott to get with the girl on the blob.

The next day me and Scott jumped on a bus to Nimbin with some Scottish girl (wee Gem's mate) to meet the Swedish boys. We all brought a shit load of weed, cookies and mushrooms, see some freaky shit and got the hell out of there to get back to Byron. When we got back Me, Scott and the Scottish, ate the mushy's and took a walk along the beach to the lighthouse. We watched the sunset and walked through the rainforest to get back, when we got back to nomadz we met up with Matty and the crew who were all fucked on different shit. We all jumped on a bus to Buddha bar to watch Matty who was on mushrooms play guitar, along with some French dude playing violin with drunken Brittany from Alabama singing, the trio absolutely smashed it! We all then took the party bus to the beach, it was team mushroom vs team acid in a game of Charades, fucking funny stuff. The next day I had to say goodbye to Byron again, I hate leaving this place, especially Matty! I am now sitting here after a hard days farming about to take shower in the river because there has been a power cut. Its crazy how fast I can go from love my life to fuck my life.

Yasoo, bookymoo, flights are booked to Thailand, 12 December which is about two weeks away, can't wait. Me and Scott are the only ones left on the farm. Lewis left last week and the Swedish left today. Lewis's last week here was pretty cool, we all had the week off. One day we took a drive to Glenyon Dam, it was beautiful, we sat by the dam with a couple of beers and a few joints watching the fisherman in the dam, and a shit load of kangaroos just meters away, hiding from the sun under trees, loads of which had joeys in their pouches. The rest of the week we would roll a few joints and take the paddle board which had an inner tube for a tractor tyre strapped to the back, so all three of us could go and float down the river. Once we were all high, we would play a game on the board, basically all stand on the board, last man standing, hours of fun. Lewis's last night was quite cool, we made a camp fire and cooked a curry in the camp stove, with freshly camped baked bread. Once dinner was over, we was all stoned watching the stars, when Greg the farmer came out on his veranda with his bagpipes, it was like being at a live gig in the Scottish highlands. Us, the audience were down by the river, high as god dam mother fuckers, and Greg about 100 feet away had the lights from the veranda shining over him, proper felt like a scene out of brave heart.

Hello there, finally our working days are over, we have a flight booked from the gold coast to Sydney, mummy farmer Lisa is going to drop us to the gold coast this Thursday. Lisa and Greg have really looked after us, this past week we have been decorating there house for a few extra bucks, and as we have been eating like kings and staying in there house for free, we have managed to save a bit of dollar. Me and Scott went to the Bonshaw x-mas party last week and all the kids I used to teach soccer to, were there. Greg dressed up as Santa Clause and arrived on the back of a Ute which was hilarious. Lisa told us that Pam Beugle (someone who Scott and Lewis done a few days' work for last week) thought they were a gay couple, I'm gutted Lewis wasn't here for the x-mas party, they could have had some fun acting gay around Pam's husband. Can't wait for Sydney, we are going to stay with Dave and Chekas who have an apartment there, as every hostel is fully booked till the new year. We are also meeting scouse Nicky in Sydney, a girl me, Scott and Matty worked with in Kavos, as well as Oscar and Noah's well awaited re-union, see you soon Matty you little Get, missed you man.

Holy, Moly, Bookie, Wookie, Cookie. I've only gone and made it back to you in one piece haven't I. Sorry if the writing is everywhere I'm on a bumpy bus in Bangkok. So the last two and half months have been fucking crazy for Matty boy. As you know me and Tommy split in Brissy to save for Thailand. I left the boys to go it alone in Byron, where I thought I could get away with the money I still have from farming. Doing good old house keeping once again, it was so weird going back alone, but fun as well. Kaia and Eline were already in Byron at the time, so was so fun meeting them

again. Before I start this I just wanna say since I haven't had this book for months this is all going by memory . . . god help me.

First night back in Byron was so fun, meeting all the new people working in Nomadz. So different, but everything is next time round, lucky for me I winged it down to Nomadz hoping for a job and got one lucky enough, they started me back straight away as night angel, which was very ironic, me telling all the drunk people coming back to be quiet. So out of the three shifts I had being night angel I worked one successfully. The first one, got too fucked because Tom came down and got excited and drunk, far too much vodka, Krista and Curtis had to put me to bed at like 1.30am. Second shift, done it all but got so high with Antonio, was a fucking funny night. Third shift, my manager took me and the other night angel out for a drink to Chunky Monkeys and got us fucked. We got back so late and forgot to do half the stuff we was meant to do. So yes moving me back to bin man was a good choice. Don't worry booky I won't tell you about every messy night in Byron because that would take forever, but there really was so many good ones. Staff parties were fucking awesome, so many funny outfits and games, like this one night we had an anything goes party. I was wearing a goon nappy filled with goon, naturally, and my body covered in nutella, was so funny getting everybody covered in it and pissing up people with my goon nappy, ha-ha.

Getting off boozing for one minute, it was great to be back at the beach and hitting the waves again and going for mad skates around Byron, I love that so much it's a joke. If I never done that during the day Byron would feel like such a waste of time, right back to the piss ups and other stuff. There was a stage some people would call a rocky patch, where certain drugs were around frequently to pop in and say hello, but if I'm honest, it was then our band created its best music, bad to say but fare in a way. As 1 guy I met called Ivan would say (you don't take drugs to be normal). So yes I had a little band in Byron with these cool guys that I met at

Nomads working, Antoine who played the violin and Brittany who sang. This was the best feeling I've ever had playing in a band, was so fitting at times, it caught me off guard and I was like shit was that us just playing. It took us about a week and a bit till we had our first gig at woody's bar, was so fun playing and being on stage. There wasn't that many people there, but we didn't care. Was just so fun playing up there after that, we started jamming a couple of times a week and started to go Buddha bar every Wednesday, which was so sick playing on a stage with loads of people watching and being pretty 'Dogs#!t' of course. Started off as a little thing then ended up making a name for ourselves for the outrageous shit that used to happen, snapping strings, getting people going mad, falling about on stage, too many drugs. I would like to say the music wasn't that bad either, and going busking was so fun as well, it was mainly down to these guys we met called Tango, Oscar, Matty and Frankie would have us out playing sing along with some goon. Then people would come out of no-where, sing and dance and act like we were out of the circus or something, was not normal busking but fun to be around. Some nights we would just jam in the stairwell and so many people would come and sing and drink, was the best feeling ever.

I also met myself a little Canadian fellow I met before in Byron but never really knew, she goes by the name of moon face (Krista). Was very weird and unexpected how we came about to like each other, but really glad it happened she is one of the nicest people I've ever met. Never sad, would do anything for anyone and being the biggest geek, she was the coolest person. Was so funny when we both worked for accommodation and both shared her bed, my bed didn't even have sheets on it. We used to hang out most days and get 'Dogs#!t' of a night, getting named the troublesome twosome by a lot of people, got a lot of time for that girl. Also broke into another festival booky, Stereosonic. Was fucking unreal, me Krista, Matilda, Tre and Rosser drove down to try and wing it, ended up walking straight in the front door with other peoples *wristbands. This one girl gave Krista little bottles of Vodka and drink tickets, what a ledge. It was pumping in there, non-stop dancing and getting water cannoned, wish Tommy was there he would have loved it, I know it. Rosser took one for the team and drove back from Brissy that night, because some of the guys had work real early in the morning, bless em. I was co-pilot in the front with Rosser but was pretty shit at it since I fell asleep most of the way home.*

So I had my 25th b-day away from work and England for a change. In Byron Bay, the best place I could ask for, Tommy couldn't make it because of work bless him, but I know we are going Thailand soon, so he was very much missed but excused. Such a good day, skating and hanging out with my buddies, had a couple of beers to. My buddy Frankie bought me this killer shirt from the op shop as a gift and I wore it all day, bloody loved it. Oh yeah not forgetting Caza who got me and Krista out of bed for a b-day Bellos and a swim in the ocean, what a cool chick. So the start of the night, the girls and Trey of room 112 decided to dress like me and wear the legendary "shits getting weird" t-shirts and even made me one out of pillow cases with b-day messages on the back in hand with a bottle of rum. I was shell shocked, so happy. One bottle of rum down, went to Buddha Bar for a b-day session, was so fun can't believe I was doing that on that day. So after partying and more rum we made our way back to Nomadz to get all the strays. Outside Nomadz there were loads of people skating and after loads of rum, I thought I was Jay Adams with 20 mins on the board I ended up stacking it and smashing my chin wide open, and needed to go hospital. Three hours later and some stiches to the chin, me and Krista tried to go back out but everything was shut, even though that happened was still the funniest and best b-day ever, fucking yeah boy.

So the day come that I had to leave good old Byron, I was gutted but at the same time I knew I was meeting the boys and going Thailand, at least I wasn't going home. Done the rounds, skated round, hung out with all my buddies and said goodbye to some people I know I won't see for a long time which sucks. Like this girl called Anna, she's like a big sister to me and by the time I get back to Oz she will be gone, so that was real hard saying by to her. So after getting some food and having one last game of civil war and beer pong with the guys, even though I'm going had to get one more of those in. So walking to the bus stop and seeing so many people I had hung around with, I was blown away by all the people standing there who I used to get wasted with. It was the worst saying by to them, I was lost for words, and I couldn't have asked for any more, I love them all. All good things must come to the end at some point I guess or paradise would not be as sweet as it is. That was some of the shizz that went down in Byron, it was some ride this time round but Thailand here we come, I'm going to try to sleep on this rocky bus ride to good old chillaxachino, look on the bright side only 10 more hours to go, see ya never.

Holy shit, where do I start, well me and Scott had an awesome last weekend in Oz, big thanks to Dave and chekas for letting us stay in their apartment, and it was great to see Nicky again. Me, Matty and Scott jumped on an Emirates plane to Bangkok, which was a scary fucking 9 hours, the turbulence was terrible, however free booze got us through it. We landed about 1am with no place to stay, so after a long walk round, piss head and prostitute infested Khoasan Road, we found our hotel, P and P Inn. A little upper class for us, but we thought we would treat ourselves, as we are only in Bangkok a few days. We all done what was needed to be done in Bangkok, see a temple, road round on a tuk tuk, got harassed by a shit load of girls in a go-go bar, feet sucked by little fish, full body massage and oh yeah got myself dreadlocks. Thought it would be funny, until I realised they were permanent extensions, oh well, can't wait to see the look on Mums face when she arrives in a few weeks. So as we were queuing for our 18 hour bus journey to koh Phangan, we noticed all the other tourists going straight upstairs, luckily for us we noticed a private booth downstairs, with a table, our own TV and enough room to lie down, happy days. So once we had a few beers, some valium and 18 hours on a bus and a ferry we arrived on koh Phangan.

We walked around the town where the full moon party is being held (Had Rin) but couldn't find anywhere to stay as everywhere was fully booked, fuck knows how, it was a ghost town. Luckily we found a place about 10 mins walk from Had Rin, we booked ourselves 3 weeks here, then all went straight to mushroom mountain for a shake. We was only going to have one shake and a quiet night, because it was so dead, but the night picked up a bit and before we knew it we was watching some amazing fire shows with some amazing people on our 3rd shake. Quiet night, yeah right, Oscar and Noah, and new recruit Sebastian (Scott) don't know how to do quiet, especially on a first night.

Ok, sorry booky I have been neglecting you, we have been on Koh phangan over two weeks and my head has been in space and my body on dance floors, so I have had to re-unite them to write something. Matty's best friend from home is here along with his travelling buddy Trevor McDonald. Oh yeah, Kaia and Eline are here as well as another 4 Norwegian Gets, so our crew is now massive. We have been out every night so far. Half-moon parties in forests, Black-moon parties on beaches, and full-moon parties in fucking space. I feel like we live here now, Had Rin beach feels like my new Barking Town Centre, and mushroom mountain is like my new Royal Oak, we are drinking the stuff by the pints. Koh Phangan is getting busier every day, this has been like a three week build up to what's going to be the greatest NYE ever. Its funny walking into the town during the day, I'm always bumping into people who say hello and know my name, but I haven't a Scooby doo, who the fucked they are. Like on x-mas day, I sat in a take away (same, same burger) and two girls came in telling me I'm a legend and how I have made their holiday. Well fuck me my nearly finished bible of awesomeness, I had no idea who these two GETS were. It's the mushy shakes, they send you on a journey so far away from reality, that when you return all those wise wisdom talkers from fairytale land are just a figment of your imagination. Plus on the other hand the five whisky buckets you drunk with the shakes get you so 'Dogs#!t', you just can't remember.

Me and the boys done secret Santa, Matty got me flip flops, I got Ash a Barbie wand, Ash got Matty a photo album, which is nice but we lost our camera last week so it's now decoration for our balcony table. Scott got John (Trevor McDonald) some fake glasses with a moustache and John got Scott breakfast the next morning because he forgot. Me and Matty got some presents from the Norwegian girls on x-mas eve, because Scandinavia celebrate x-mas on the 24th, weirdo's if you ask me, but it means we had two x-mas's which was handy because me and Scott are used to having two x-mas's.

Ok Mr. bookmiestro, Koh Phangan has been fucking out of control, with x-mas done and 20 billion shroom shakes drunk the long awaited NYE is here. I'm sitting here in this cool bar called sunset bar, the best chill out spot on the Island reflecting on these last couple of weeks. I can safely say me, Tommy and Scott have tried every mushroom this place has to offer and the nights here are simply unexplainable unless you were there and hi as fuck. You have your mixture of everyone here, weirdo's, roid heads, sniffer dogs, the list goes on, it's safe to say this is the craziest and weirdest party I've ever attended and hopefully live to see it through till NYE. I don't want to end up eating a Thai red curry on my own again at 4am, I mean who does that, a little sit down meal in Mr. K's restaurant having a nice little dinner, stupid sexy shrooms.

Sawadee Kup, Mr. Book, ya big fuck. NYE full-moon party was fucking awesome. We had the biggest three week pre-party for it, and was worth the wait. The countdown was wicked, we were altogether as it went off. 70 thousand people on one beach, all getting off with each other and all kinds of crazy shit. I bumped into so many people that night from home and travelling. I didn't stop partying until 4pm New Year's Day. I ended up in mushy mountain with a load of randoms watching a monsoon slowly approach, that's when I called it a day.

So we woke up 6am on the 2nd of January to go through a journey from hell. The monsoon was still going strong, as we got a three hour boat to mainland. Once we survived the boat trip, we then got two coaches that took in total with all the fucking waiting around 7 hours to get to Phuket airport where we met mum. Apart from feeling like absolute horseshit, it was good seeing mum. We got a cab to Patong beach, walked around for two hours looking for a place to stay as everything was fully booked, but finally found somewhere. The next day we woke up and went straight to the beach, weather is finally good. We had a go on some jet skis then went elephant trekking which was scary but fun. That night we all went out for a drink, but it wasn't really a late one, I think I had more fast food than beer. The next morning we got a mini-bus to the port and jumped on a two hour boat to Koh Phi Phi, this boat was heaven compared to our last one. We got to Phi Phi just after midday which wasn't good as once again everything was fully booked. We checked into our really nice resort just for one night until we found something cheaper. Really regret not staying there as our next place we paid five nights for was shocking, shower stunk of Kavos and the beds were rock solid, oh well, ya win some ya loose some.

We have met up with everyone from Koh Phangan, it feels like the NYE build up all over again, daytime drinking with all sorts of weird shit going down. Like the other day we was all talking about how we was going to start a boat party on an abandoned ship we named "Jenny". My mum was going to be the DJ (Dj Fomo), and the rest of us were going to promote it. The next day it actually happened, loads of people turned up, it was so funny. Today we all rented out 6 or 7 kayaks, and rowed to monkey beach, love that beach, probably the 6th time I've been to that beach, ya can never get bored of it.

Shapnin booknam, ya little kup kup, I'm coming to the end of my holidays, aint I, well gutted. Phi Phi was awesome, the weather was spot on, getting myself nice and brown for our Aussie return. Mum loves it out here, she has loved all our travelling buddies and our adventurous days out. Especially the Phi Phi boat trip to a deserted island, as well as Maya Bay (where the beach was filmed), heaps of snorkeling, another monkey beach and a sunset we watched on a long boat. Don't think we appreciated it as much as we should because we were all 'Dogs#!t', but 18 people on a longboat getting smashed was great. We had a good few nights out on Phi Phi, another full moon party, there wasn't 70 thousand people this time but still good fun with a load of GETS, fire shows and bars you can smoke weed in. Our last night on Phi Phi we all went to reggae bar, inside the bar there is a boxing ring you can fight in for a free bucket. So Kaia and Kristine had a fight as well as me and Scott, couldn't really breathe properly after, but worth a free bucket.

Me, Scott, Matty and Mum left everyone to get an hour boat ride to Koh Lanta for my birthday and last days in Thailand. The weather hasn't been the greatest, but it's just what the doctor ordered, an amazing resort, with hot showers, comfy beds, a swimming pool, a restaurant facing the sunset every evening and a bar that sells weed and mushrooms. This resort is in the middle of no-where, with a beach one side and a rainforest the other. On my birthday 7 Norwegian girls, Eline, both Kaia's, Kristine, Tuva, Brigette and her fella Paul, Mina and her parents all came to the same resort. I'm so glad because Kaia and Eline who me and Matty travelled the east coast of Oz with were flying back to Norway, not like a few of their friends who are going to Oz after Thailand. So it could possibly be a goodbye and not just see ya later. Today was a great last day together, we all got in the back of a pick-up truck/tuk tuk to have an hours elephant trekking through the rainforest, and trek up the waterfalls and caves, it was an amazing day. Now just sitting here about to get ready for our last night in Lanta, so 'lets get Dogs#!t'.

Ya hoo, the book of many mysteries, so the last night with everyone in Lanta has come, we all started at the bar in the resort, got a few buckets in and then all decided to branch out and go to another bar, not that there's many to choose from. So 15 of us get in a tuk tuk, yes that's right many many people darling. Ended up at this random bar where a Thai rock band is playing, was weird but fun, I tried asking if I could go up and play but the guy just looked at me with a blank face and was like no way, good decision, I think. So we ended up getting a load of snacks and headed back to the apartment and more beers of course, and just continued getting 'Dogs#!t' till early hours even though me and the boys had an early bus in the morning. Fuck it ay! After a long ass bus we made it back into Phuket, where we had to say a farewell goodbye to Tommy's mum, bless her. She has been a trooper this whole trip, never missed out on anything and was up for everything, she loved our stories and wanted some good ones of her own to take home. Even though she's the boys mum she felt like mummy number two for me. D J Fomo you legend. So chilling out for a couple of days in the middle of nowheresville with no drinks just snacks and sleep. We packed our shit and had our last Thailand cab to the airport for our long quest to Perth. It was so sad to say bye to Thailand, but I'm really excited for Aussie round part 2. Got a real good feeling about this second time round even though we are more skint than ever, ha-ha it will be alright just have something to eat.

Yes yes my little bad boy biography, what a fucking journey it has been. We got to Phuket airport 5 hours early to pay our fine for over staying our visa and didn't want to miss the flight. Luckily the process was pretty quick, just a bit of banter with some Thai immigration officer who couldn't speak a word of English. Then we boarded a two hour flight to Singapore, where we then spent 16 hours for our connecting flight to Perth. Singapore airport is huge, so we took a long walk round, spending most of our time taking photos in some massive angry birds Photo display, then found some kids jungle gym to sleep in and around for the night. After the worst night's sleep we boarded our 6 hour flight to Perth. The flight was a bit of a shit one because there was no free booze, but the view from the plane was amazing. On the left you could see a thunderstorm and on the right a beautiful sunset on the clearest sky.

Finally back in Oz, wwwooooooo. Instead of wasting money on a nights rent, we slept in the airport, the reason being is that we aint got a pot to piss in, plus we just like sleeping in airports. We got a bus into the city and went straight to the hospital because Scott's disease which he caught through tea-bagging a lady boy in Thailand was getting worse. He got his cream and pills and they started working straight away, thank fuck because he started to look like elephant man, then we checked into the worst hostel in Oz. Everywhere was fully booked, only booked one night, and left our bags in the hostel storage, and was going to just sleep in the TV room, until we found somewhere else. But it got to about 11pm and the hostel was getting quiet and empty, so we decided to get another hostel. We found our new home international backpackers, which was fucking sweet, they had room with free breakfast, close to the city and across the road from the blue-cat bus route. Nicky our friend from Kavos got a train from Adelaide to meet us here, we all got on the case of job searching, and spent most of our days down that fucking library for free internet. The job search was looking pretty grim as it is so busy in Perth and every backpacker we met was looking for work. We bumped into two friends we met in Thailand Jim and Bolly, they are in the same boat as us skint and looking for work. It is so fucking hot here at the moment, we all took a bus to Scarborough beach and I burnt my head really bad, because I've had my dread's cut out and the top of my head hasn't seen sun since 2010. The beach was amazing with some cool waves to fuck around in. We also took a day trip to Freemantle beach, not as nice and there were loads of jellyfish, but we watched an amazing sunset with a few boxes of goon. Yesterday was a good day, it was Australia day. We started off drinking on the balcony then took a picnic and a few boxes of goon to Kings Park. This park is up on a hill that looks over the city, there was an awesome air show followed by fireworks, we ended up going to some proper freaky random club, wicked night. Today I had a phone call that saved our bacon, it's a job picking grapes on a vineyard for all 6 of us, all we need is a car, hopefully an old friend of Matty's who lives in Perth is going to let us borrow his car for a few months as he didn't need it, so fingers crossed.

Well I tell ya what don't ever bother crossing ya fingers, ya only gonna give yourself cramp. Anything free is too good to be true, I will explain why. So we woke up Saturday morning, all checked out of our hostels and started to organise the journey to the vineyard in Margaret River which is 300 k south of here. Me, Scott and Jim got a bus to Matty where he was staying at his friend's house. We got there and Joe Matty's mate told us the car wouldn't start, so we all give it a push start and the car (Larry the Laser) only bloody started, so Scott drove the car back to the city where Nicky and Bolly were waiting with our camping equipment. On the way there the car kept cutting out, luckily some Aussie dude we met called Brian was a mechanic, and he told us if we change the water hose and drained the shit petrol it would be fine. So as the car would literally not start, me and Scott took a train to a place that sold spare parts, while the rest of the guys looked after the car as it was in a no parking zone and all of our shit was in it. Me and Scott walked about 3 miles in the 42 degree heat, to find out the guys got a second opinion from another mechanic and he said the head gasket was gone, which basically meant it was a waste of a fucking walk as the car is fucked. So we then got back to the car to then discover Aussie Brian standing by the car and was adamant the head gasket was fine, but by this time all the shops were closed and didn't get any spare parts, fucking fuming. We all then made a decision to stay in Perth one more night so we could get the parts tomorrow. We had to empty the car of all our stuff because it was parked in drunken aboriginal central. So Me, Jim, Nicky and

Bolly checked back into hostels, and Matty and Scott went back to Joes. In the morning Jim and the girls jumped on a train to meet us there because we couldn't all fit in the car, and Scott and Matty met me at the car with the spare parts. We managed to fit the parts and hit the road, just before we got to the motorway the car started to cut out. As we pulled back into the city Larry the laser cut out right behind an RAC van. The mechanic in the RAC van said to us it must be the shit petrol in the car, which was something we were told just forgot to do. Could this weekend get any fucking better, well it just so happens no it fucking cant. On the way to the petrol garage, after breaking down at every traffic light in Perth's CBD, our car came to its final stop, followed by the scariest sound, it started smoking from the bonnet and sounded like it was going to explode. We all got out the car as fast as possible, unfortunately for me, my door didn't open, so I superman dived out of the window and landed on my knee, we phoned the fire brigade as the noise and smoke was getting worse, just before fireman Sam and co turned up, the car give an almighty bang and stopped smoking. It was a really scary experience, as not only did I think I was going to die, and completely busted my knee but our whole lives was in that car. Fireman Sam opened up the bonnet to discover the radiator had exploded, so we said goodbye to Larry the deathtrap laser and got on a bus to Margaret River. To be honest the bus journey was nice, but nice buses wasn't making me happy, due to the fact that I now look like forest Gump and we were going to a camp site with no car, which was a necessity because the camp site is nowhere near the vineyard, well its only 5 k but when you walk like John Wayne, it's hard.

Journal 2

So here he is! Book of mysteries, numero 2. So it's been a week and a bit since we last met and there's been a couple of things I need to tell ya. So as you know we was all in a bit of bother in Perth being skint, homeless and a little bit more skint. Our savior there was my friend joey who I use to work with back in England a long time ago, he was wicked man, when things were shit he put us up, gave us some proper food, no noodles, and even gave us a free ride, which blew up but was a nice offer. It was so good to see him after all these years, you're the man Joey. So after all the kerfuffle with the car, we jumped on a bus to Maggy River, and this bus was like no other. It had its own Wi-Fi, plug sockets, big ass seats, the lot.

It was a very pleasant ride all the way there, we pulled up to our campsite with our newly acquired tents and made it feel like home as we were gonna be here for a while. The only thing we have got to get use to again, is getting up farm time, 6 o clock bitches, it sucks to be us. First day grape picking wasn't actually that bad, we started early and finished early like 1 o clock, so plenty of time to see the wicked beaches W.A has to offer. The main problem with grapes is that you don't get a lot of money per bucket so you have to snip your heart out just to make a couple of bucks. The funniest part is watching this guy called qui, do his speech every morning and constantly forgetting what he's even going on about, except the 8km speed limit he never forgets that.

We have had a lot of days off at the moment because of the weather, so we have taken advantage of what the campsite has to offer and the new car we have. DEVLIN. Scotty even towed me on the back of it on my skateboard. The hills round here are sick for skating, love them, and the waves are unreal, like big pieces of awesomeness. So our days off are coming to an end and the grapes are ready for our snips. Which is a good thing because mine and Tommy's tab is getting ridiculous.

But soon we should have enough grape money to rule the world.

Hello new book, so the first journal is over, gonna miss that little black bastard. With all due respect Mr. new book, and I'm saying with all due respect, but your brown in colour and falling to bits, so don't get the ump when I finally type you up on my laptop and throw you in the bin. Well Gracetown Caravan Park has been fucking sweet, it's cheap and bang in the middle of all the vineyards. Every Wednesday and Saturday they put on a movie on the outdoor cinema screen, as well as lots of other free shit, like tennis, basketball, volleyball, and laundry. South West Australia is beautiful, there are loads of beaches with awesome surf and plenty of marine life for a little snorkel, the small very wealthy towns are surrounded by immaculate wineries and vineyards. This is definitely a place I would advise anyone to retire in. After a lot of searching and fucking about, Scott and Nicky, who are the only ones with any money, bought a car (DEVLIN), it's a sweet little run around. After our week off due to bad weather, because a cyclone just missed us, we have been hardcore grape picking. It aint that bad to be honest, it's just that we only work 3-4 hours a day, so we aint gonna be able to save as much as we wanted. Plus I've had a spot of bother back home with my flat, and owe a bit more money than I thought, so I really need to start job searching for better paid jobs in Perth.

It's a shame because I really do like it here, especially days like today. After work we all jumped in Devlin and drove 20k north of here to a place called Yallingup, it was breathtaking. We climbed down these rocks, which is hard for me at the moment as I've got big blisters on both my feet from playing Tennis barefoot. But the climb was worth it. On one side you could see a beautiful untouched beach with some god dam sexy surf surrounded by sand dunes that would be sick for sand boarding, and on the other side there is a waterfall which is made by the Indian Ocean smashing over the rocks. It was wicked to sit on the top and get smashed by these waves, it was like a real life water park. At the bottom of the little waterfall, the pool there, was like a spa, the water was crystal clear filled with tropical fish that then backed onto a natural whirlpool which you could cliff jump into. We met our friends from the vineyard there Sam and Kat, and Sam had a spear for fishing, he caught himself a few fish, pukka little tool, it was spring loaded attached to your wrist. I didn't like it when he poked the snake we see on the way back to the cars, I'm sure that snake give me a look to say "if you don't stop that Muppet poking me, I'm gonna cut him". Anyway, it was an awesome day.

Wot shapnin new book. A few weeks have past and a lot has changed. I've left Maggy River, and gone back to Perth in search for some better paid work. Matty, Scott and Nicky are going to stay and stick it out and pick the rest of the grapes. They do have a tent each now, due to me Bolly and Jim all leaving. Bolly and Jim were in a relationship going nowhere fast, so after a lot of arguing and stress, Bolly packed her bags and left for Perth, shortly after Jim also left booking his flight back to England. I've been in Perth nearly a week and the job searching is not going great, so I've started to look elsewhere for work, and by the looks of it the best place to look is Sydney. I've checked back into my old hostel, where Bolly is staying as well. Bolly is so amazing, she is the cutest, sweetest girl I know, with a heart of gold. The more I'm with Bolly the more I think I'm falling for her. After this week me and nana Bolly have become really close, so close in fact we booked a flight together for Sydney. I'm so fucking excited right now, I can't wait to see the back of Perth and to start fresh in Sydney, just me and Bolly.

Mr. new book of justice, I've always believed in fate, as my journey in life has taken me down some strange paths but always works out for the best and I have such a good feeling about this. I know I haven't known Bolly long, and in the back of my mind think I could be just a rebound from Jim, but the feelings I'm getting are something more than I've ever had, I can only hope she feels the same.

Holy shit my little old mukka, these past few weeks have been . . . . Well shits getting weird. Mine and Bolly's last night in Perth was a good one, everyone from the hostel treated themselves to a sneaky pill. We all had a drink on the balcony and then dropped the little fellas. It was jokes watching everyone come up in the first bar. One by one you could see everyone slowly starting to dance and before you knew it, we were all up on the dance floor. Epic night.

The next day we packed our stuff said by to everyone and got on our bus to the airport. We arrived in Sydney at 7am, got a bus straight to Bondi, had a little nap on the beach, and then checked into Noah's Ark Backpackers. I couldn't stop laughing when they give us room 202, such a legendary room. All day we spent job searching and flat hunting, one job that phoned back was a farming job in Gatton, near Brisbane. After a lot of debate we decided to buy a car with the little money we had and drive up to the farm. So the next day me and Bolly walked round the city and pretty much covered it all in one day. That afternoon is when we were introduced to our beloved "Rodney", the car. The

Toyota Corolla was a good little runner with rego till October and only 160,000k on the clock, the only thing wrong was the front right headlight. Someone had reversed into good old rodders a few weeks back, we wasn't too bothered because it still worked, so we drove back to Bondi to pick up our stuff. As we were having our pizza hut in the car before we hit the road, the exposed headlight blew. So now it was dark and we had no lights. Fucking perfect, that's just what you need when trying to dodge kangaroos on the road, so we decided to sleep in the car for the night until the sun came up. So bright and early we started our trip. We didn't have a map so we kind of guessed our way up the coast. We decided to drive to Byron Bay and stay there a few nights.

The 15 hour drive to Byron was awesome, we got to drive over Sydney Harbour Bridge which was cool and took a few little detours on the way up. Me and Bolly were feeling a bit grimey because we haven't had a shower since yesterday morning, so we drove through this lovely little town called Glouster and came across an outdoor swimming pool with showers. Rodney is like a sweat box, so this swim was like the best idea. As we were getting closer to Byron the sun was slowly fucking off and with no headlights we were getting worried. We stopped at a garage and found a bulb that fit, but for some reason the only way the lights came on was if Bolly held the stick back as if you put on your full beams. To be quite honest with you, we didn't want to sleep in the car by the side of the road in Oz bush, I've seen the movie Wolf Creek and it's not fun at all. So Bolly said she didn't mind holding the stick while she drove, however good old rodders decided to shine both his lights without holding anything, happy days. So we made it to Byron safe and sound with enough time to get a box of goon before the bottle shop closed. We managed to find a sweet parking spot away from the busy town so we could get some sleep in the car. It was a lovely night, we laid on the bonnet watching the most perfect night sky. As we sat in the car having a glass of goon, a police car pulled up next to us. They asked us what we were doing, so we told them having a night cap before we sleep in our mobile home, they just grinned and fucked off, it was sweet, I think they were looking for weed, or maybe the police woman just wanted my bits because she was a proper little GET.

The next day we both went into Nomadz to use their showers, and I bumped into so many old faces. Me and Bolly had a chat with Matilda and my old supervisor Sandy who Matilda now lives with and they politely asked us to stay at their house till we hit the road again. As much as we felt bad, we really needed this, I mean bless Rodders he means well but not comfy one bit. So we drove to Nimbin for a few hours until the girls finished work, it was wicked. I've only ever been to Nimbin by coach, but driving is so much better, it's an amazing drive, the countryside is beautiful. When you drive to Nimbin it's pretty much all uphill and the view back down is amazing, words and pictures cannot describe the beauty of it. When we got to Nimbin we bought a bag of weed, and smoked the biggest joint. It was so funny, I had such bad dry mouth and really needed a drink and it was making Bolly laugh so much. But she was too paranoid to walk back into town with me to get a drink because she couldn't stop giggling, one of them had to be there moments, but it was jokes. We drove back to Sandy's house, had some dinner and a few drinks, and then went out.

It was a wicked night, we started off in the Rails watching a live band then went to Nomadz to top up on goon, then had a boogie in Woopy's and ended up at Chunky Monkeys, the whole night was pretty much free as I still know the doorman and bartenders. The following day, we spent the whole day on the beach. I bumped into the Norwegian girls from Thailand, it was so good to see them again. Once we got back to the house we got invited to a BBQ by the beach with all the housemates. Some French dude (the violinist from Matty's little band), had his family over and it was them who hosted the BBQ. It was a really nice evening, we were all up singing and dancing to a load of French songs, so funny. The next day Me, Bolly, Matilda, Kaia and Tuva all drove to Brisbane to sneak into Future Music Festival, and success it was. We managed to get a wristband each off of the people leaving the festival, then blagged to the front desk that we had to come out to help our friend into a taxi because he was too drunk, it was jokes we literally got escorted to the front gate. Got to see some amazing acts, Swedish House Mafia, Skrillex, Sven Vath and many more. Apart from it pissing down at the end and the long wet drive home, it was a good night.

Wot shapnin book, so I'm on another farm, can't get enough of these farms. We drove to a place called Gatton in Queensland, the house we got is fucking sweet. Me and Bolly have got our own room, with carpet, wardrobes, the lot. The housemates are interesting to say the least. There's an Irish dude who smokes weed when he finishes work, he has been blazing on his own, but luckily for him me and Bolly are here to help. We spent 5 days in this house waiting to be told where we are going to work. We both done a day's gardening for our landlord for a bit of cash and to pass time, as all we have been doing with our time is getting on the goon. So one morning Ken the Landlord tells us we will be picking Capsicum down in a town called Warwick, we was both meant to start on Wednesday, but there was a spot for one to start on Saturday, so I have been split up from Bolly as I've just done my first days picking. It's not that bad just a bit back aching, and our new house is even sweeter than the last, we have our own room again, with a comfier bed, but I'm on my own because Bolly doesn't get here till Tuesday, proper miss her already, I'm sure she is having fun up in Gatton gardening and smoking with Irish. This weekend away from each other might do us good as we have been in each other's pockets since we left Perth, and things did start to get a bit tense, with not having any money or work. However we have a new house, a new job and Rodney is still going strong, really can't wait to see Bolly again, miss that little get.

Well well well if it isn't my book of magic, a week has pasted and I have moved another 2 times. I finished my 3rd day picking Capsicum awaiting Bollys return, but on Tuesday night our landlord Mayla (Ken's wife) turned up and told me I had to go back to Gatton, because Bolly is now working for her full time supervising the backpackers, so Mayla sorted me out a job chasing chickens in Gatton so we can be together. I was happy to be re-united with Bolly but was gutted to leave Warwick as I was just getting settled. My chicken chasing job is jokes, apart from the fact they keep shitting, puking and spraying period blood all over me, it's a lot of fun.

After my first day fucking around with chicken Joe and friends, I got back to the house to discover we have to move again, so now me and Bolly are living in a new house with 2 German guys and 2 English girls, it's the size of a shoe box, but a nice little gaff. We have our own room again and because of the little perks to Bollys job our fridge and freezer is full. Couldn't be happier at the moment, love my new house and job, and me and Bolly are getting closer and more compassionate every day. Its paddy's day today and everyone from my Warwick house is coming up to get 'Dogs#!t' with us, happy days.

Fuck me, reading that last paragraph could not have been more than the truth, it's funny how 1 night can change everything. So paddy's day begun and we all started getting on it. Everyone from Warwick came down as well as the guys from Mayla court road, plus 4 random Swedish dudes who just moved in next door. Everyone ended up in our house, which wasn't good because it's the size of a shoebox, so we took a walk to a house Bolly knew was empty, it was in this house that shit hit the fan. There was a lot of shit stirring going on by everyone about me and Bolly and our relationship status, and gooned up to the max reacted to all the rumours like a fucking child. I ended up in the toilet of this house party with one of the English girls from our house, acting naughty, and guess who was outside waiting to go to the toilet, yes Bolly. I've never had my heart drop into my balls like that before. I was so pissed, didn't realize I had done anything wrong, and just kept thinking of the things that Bolly was meant to have said about me. I'm a fucking arsehole, as much as I know all the shit stirring was probably true, should never have reacted the way I did. So once being caught red handed with some dog from Essex, I left the party, went home, packed my bags and started hitchhiking somewhere.

I've got to be the biggest mug, goon is a naughty drink and it's taken me a long time to figure out. I was hitchhiking down a country lane in the bush of Oz with $100 in my sky rocket, luckily no random weirdo picked me up. I ended up walking back to Gatton and sleeping on a random sofa in the house down Mayla court road. I woke up so fucking confused about what had happened last night, there were people from the party awake in this house filling me in everything that happened. I just wanted to die right there and then, luckily got passed on a spliff which helped, and just booked myself a bus to Brisbane. On the way to the bus stop, I phoned my chicken boss to let him know I wouldn't be in, and he told me to come stay with him so I at least had a job. Which was a fucking wise move as I aint got a pot to piss in.

My new house mate some English dude called Joe picked me up and took me to my new house. I met my new house mates, 2 Irish dudes Kristian and Power, Belgium Simon and some Canadian chick Hayley. After my last days chicken chasing and first days Potato picking, I'm now sitting in a new house wondering what the fuck has just happened this last month. I miss Bolly a lot but nothing can be done to mend things between us, even though these past few weeks have been amazing, regret leaving the guys on the west coast. Do ya know what new book, I think you might be more interesting than the last. Don't get me wrong me and the first book of justice had a fucked up year, but 2012, its one for the history books.

Oi Oi booky, where you been hiding. It's been about a month since we last spoke, and yeah still on a farm, picking poxy potatoes, but what a pukka little month it's been. Loving my new gaff and housemates, apart from crack head Hayley everyone I live with works with me on potatoes. All the guys make the job worth doing, if we didn't have a laugh whilst doing it I would go insane. After work we all have a good smoke as Power is the supplier, which has come in handy but dangerous for my savings. The local pub is a good crack, you end up seeing other backpackers working in Gatton down there, I aint seen silly bollox down there yet (Bolly), but I know she's found herself a Swedish dude to keep her busy. Ahh bless her, good luck to her, she's a big div but aint a bad little tart.

I was getting a bit worried about her not giving me the money for my half of the car, but on the day my boss tells me I've got the week off work, she come round with the money. So I thought fuck it and went Byron Bay for a week. It was mental. I woke up early on Wednesday and got a bus and 2 trains to Brisbane. I was gonna hitchhike from Brissy to Byron, but got in touch with some Canadian chick I met in Perth and she let me stay round hers for the night because she wanted to come to Byron with me. She lived with a Brazilian bird, 2 Spanish dudes, a French couple and an Italian guy. It was hilarious listening to them all try and talk English to each other, bloody hopeless, nice people though. Eilish (Canada) and Anna (Brazilian), were in the same boat as me, going Byron with no accommodation or travel booked, on its busiest weekend, it's the weekend blues festival is in town. Last year's Blues Fest—Easter weekend was a good one, and this one equally went down a treat. I have a lot of friends in Byron, so accommodation for me wasn't an issue but I was now with 2 random chicks. Luckily Kaia and Tuva, 2 Norwegian girls I met in Thailand had a house share in Byron and they were up for coming Blues fest.

Me, Eilish and Anna got a lift off of some random dude we found on the website Gumtree down to Byron. We dumped our bags round Kaia and Tuvas and started drinking. Matty boy came over with Matilda and a few others and we all got the bus to Blues fest. Our intensions were to go for the easy option and wait for people to leave to get there wristbands, but we got fucked early and tried sneaking in. Unfortunately there were 15 of us, and we all stuck out like a sore thumb. So failing to get in we decided to go back to Byron for a night out, bit of a blurry night, but me and Matty were last men standing at some not so busy beach party, I ended up staying round some Swedish girls house Anna, you may remember her she was Matilda's travelling buddy. It was a pukka first day and night in Byron, there are so many people still here who I met in Byron last year as well as others I've met in Oz and Thailand. Sagapo re-unions.

The next day I was chilling on the beach with the girls and Scotty phones me and said that he sold his car and booked a flight to the gold coast and will be in Byron in the morning, about time I've missed that big gimp. That night was another goodun, we all went to a house party, then to Nomadz for a few drinking games, then hit Aquarius bar, Chunky Monkeys and Woopy's. I bumped into Steve in Woopy's, he's an old family friend from England. Luckily I made it back to Kaia and Tuva's gaff this night because I was meeting Scott there in the morning.

It's so good to see Scott again, he's gonna join me on the farm in Gatton. It was good to hear his stories about the grape farm on the west, and to tell him about my random adventure. After spending another day on the beach with Scott, Matty and the crew, we all went for a shit, shave, shower and met up in the owl and pussycat bar before going Nomadz for drinking games. Anna the

Brazilian bless her was getting proper stitched up, her English is so bad. It was this night I got a phone call from Bolly, having a go at me because she was in Byron and her car had been smashed up. It was laughable, I'm 26 years old having the time of my life with friends and family, the last thing on my mind was vandalizing some little girl's car. She was obviously upset by what happened, and the fact that I was in Byron at the time she didn't know who else to blame. It's a shame because I did still want to stay friends with her, but she can go suck on a gingernut now I know she thinks I would do something as childish as this.

Me, Scott, Canada and Brazil were meant to get up early and hitchhike back to Brissy, but Canada got a phone call from the dude who dropped us down here and was driving back through to Brissy, so the girls got in with him. However me and Scott stayed as we was already too late to make it back to Gatton from Brissy and would rather spend the night in Byron than Brissy. So I phoned my boss to let him know we wouldn't be back to work in the morning and he said how we wasn't needed for an extra day anyways, so we had another day to get back, happy days. Now the 'let's get dogs#!t' levels can be raised without feeling too guilty.

I'm glad we stayed that extra night because it was a lot of people in Byron's last night and was nice to say goodbye to a lot of people. The journey back to the farm the next day was a killer, instead of a 2 hour drive to Brissy we got a 4 hour bus, and instead of an hour drive from Brissy to Gatton we got 2 trains and a bus which took 3 hours. Just what you need after a weekend that involved, half a dozen Pixie caps, litres of Goon, and a heavy smoke. It was the first time me and Scott were pleased to be back on a farm.

How's it going shit cunt, terrible language I know but that's Australia for ya, especially out here in the bush. People round here say things like "eat shit, ya shit cunt", instead of good morning. I thought my cockney slang had a lot of swear words in it, fuck, I'm well—spoken round here. Anyway my little book of weird and wonderful thoughts, a few more weeks have past and life as a farmer in gatton aint been too sad. A friend of mine from home Lauren got in touch with me on fb and told me she had a friend in Oz looking for farm work. So I put her onto my boss and within a few days she and four other girls turned up. It was sweet. There were five blokes living in our house, which is cool, but five new girls was a blessing. The first day they all went through the house and cleaned everything. Don't get me wrong we kept it nice and tidy, but these girls got on their hands and knees scrubbing shit, happy days. Unfortunately three of the girls left a week later, because they wasn't promised enough work, and needed money more than a second years visa, while the two Irish girls Orla and Leanne stayed. It was a shame because all ten of us were getting on really well, but to be perfectly honest with ya, I never got to see the bathroom is was constantly in use, so it wasn't a bad idea them fucking off after all.

Now there's seven of us in this gaff which is the perfect amount for how big it is. We have been doing allsorts together after work. Badminton on Thursdays, football pretty much every other day, we got a nice little family going on. Belgium Simon left last week, and Pommy Joe is leaving this week, so me and Scott will be living with four Irish, god help us. Only kidding there a good crack. Work is picking up as well, we was only working four days a week on potatoes, but now we are doing two days a week on chickens as well, so loving the six day weeks at the moment. The more work the better as we both want, as much money saved as possible by the end of June to get the hell out of here and start a new adventure. Our plan is to buy a car drive to Darwin via Ayres rock, then fly to Bali for a cheeky week's holiday, followed by a long drive to cairns and down the east coast all the way to Byron Bay. However plans change all the time as you well know Mr. Book. I mean I could meet a girl, buy a car and end up in a complete new city, like a fucking tit that I am, like fuck, I've learnt from my mistakes. Talking of mistakes, I've been seeing Bolly a lot more recently, I think Scotts kind of been an ice breaker for us, which is good because she seems down and I wouldn't want her to think she couldn't just come round and hang out with us, bless her. I skype'd everyone from home yesterday, Mum, Dad, all the boys, even Pops. It was so good to see them all. I bloody miss home a lot, I've been away seventeen months now and honestly have no idea when I will return, or if I will return. I feel like backpacking is my life now, and don't want it to end.

What's the crack? Long time no see me old mukka, I've had a really good couple of weeks. Work has been too sweet. I've had one day off in three weeks and still going, savings are doing really well. The chicken job is so easy it's a joke. Like today for example, we were tightening nuts and bolts whilst getting high and getting paid good money for it. We have a right laugh on both our jobs. On chickens there are ten of us all Irish and English, that are slowly putting together a shit load of chicken cages, and when I say slowly I mean slowly. On potatoes it's me and Scott on one team, and Nat and Nathan on the other, we are the pickers. We are always winding the northerners up, because we beat them every time. We have actually got a bet on for the last day picking, and it's a race to see who can pick the most spuds whilst in women's clothes.

Last weekend Me, Scott, Bolly and Power drove to Brisbane, picked up Canadian Eilish and drove to Byron to do a skydive. Unfortunately the weather was shitty, so couldn't jump, as gutted as we were, we were happy to just go Nimbin, get high and stock up on supplies. We got back to Byron, ate all the mushys and went on a little trek to the lighthouse, we done the coastal walk down to the beach and watched some of the surfers at sunset, it turned out to be an awesome day, skydive or not. Luckily power didn't do any mushys, so he drove home, but he's driving was terrible, it was a scary four hour journey home.

Booky Boy, how's it hanging, guess what, I'm no longer farming. Oh mate, what a great feeling it is. We was meant to stay a few weeks more, but I acted like a retard the other day and ripped a tendon in my arm, so I can't work, as I'm in a sling again, let's just say it was surfing again. So me and Scotty went to Brissy and bought a car, he's name is Sebastian the Subaru. Good old Seb, he has got to get us to Darwin by the 17th July as we have booked flights to Bali for that date. Our past few weeks in Gatton have been such a laugh, there have been loads of house party's that involved all the backpackers in town, everyone we have met have been so good. Leanne and Orla, were getting fed up every night with me and Scott arguing who will make the lunches for work. So the girls proposed a deal, if they make our lunches, we had to buy their weekly goon. It was going ok, until Nat and Nathan started getting better lunches from the girls in their house, they were getting massage tokens, homemade cakes, the lot. So of course me and Scott had a little moan and things improved.

Our last night in Gatton was a good one, all the girls made a roast dinner for mine and Scotts leaving do. They cooked for over 15 people, and some of the guys there, can fucking eat, trust me. It was a great send off, really gonna miss everyone. For weeks now me and Scott ave been gagging for a good night out, and that weekend we bought the car was a bank holiday (Queens Birthday), so we went to a club called the Met. It was just what the doctor ordered, good music, GETS everywhere, and a few little naughty ones to get us going. It was funny, at the end of the night the bouncers had to pretty much tell us to leave, as we were the last three people dancing.

Today we drove the car to Texas to see our old farmers Greg and Lisa for the evening. It wasn't on our route, but they looked after us last year, so it's nice to make an effort. We have just got back from fishing, Greg let us take his boat down the river with his rods, love this family, always trying to please people. We have got dinner round here tonight, then driving to surfers paradise tomorrow, which is going to be sick, as the girls that turned up to

Gatton and left after a week are working in a hostel there, so there will be a place to crash as well as mass spoonage.

Hello book ya big shit, proper loving this road trip. We left surfers paradise after a messy night out with the girls and drove seven hours north to rainbow beach. We stopped off in Noosa to grab some lunch on the way. Noosa is a beautiful part of the sunshine coast, it's a shame it was just a fly by visit, we managed to get to rainbow beach before sunset, which was handy because it's a fucker trying to cook and set up the car in the dark. All over Australia you have 'rest areas' for people in caravans, campervans or camper cars like Sebastian, and nine times out of ten have showers and places to cook. We woke up and had breakfast in our rest area that was literally on the beach facing Fraser Island, too fucking sweet. We then drove up to the sand dunes to get some decent pictures, as so far we have fuck all pictures, we then spent the rest of the day getting high.

The next morning we carried on heading north and ended up staying at a rest area looking over a huge Dam. We got convinced to stay in this place because it said it had a golf course, but once we found out it was a nine hole crazy golf built by a blind man, it was too late to move on. Fuck it, it had decent showers and power points for the laptop. We hit the road in the morning and arrived in 1770, just after mid-day. We cooked up some lunch by the beach and was planning to stay there the night. But after a few hours on the beach, we still had plenty of daylight left, so we hit the road and spent the night just outside Mackay. It's funny we don't use time anymore, we just keep an eye on the sun, so we can get plotted up before dark. The following day we drove inland to Emerald. This is where Matty boy was working in some bottle shop next to a pub. It was so good to see him again. The night we got there, was some special event called bombs away at the pub. So as you do, we got 'Dogs#!t' and raved it up with Matty and his lovely girlfriend Caz. It weren't a bad night, music was pretty decent, but the pub was full of a load of meat headed miners, as Emerald is a big mining town. After I think the fourth time this year saying by to Matty, we drove to Airlie Beach.

Yes finally in the tropics, no more cold nights. We got in touch with an old friend we met in Byron last year. Krista the Canadian. She and some Aussie dude were in Airlie looking for work, travelling in some cool Mercedes van that the dude had pimped out into a campervan. We met up with them and had a good couple of nights out in Airlie beach. The morning we were going to leave, we all had a BBQ for breakfast and it's was then the guys decided to tag along the trip. They couldn't find any work in Airlie so decided to drive to Cairns with us, by the time we get to Darwin, we could have our own camper travel 'Hells Angels Crew'. So all four of us took a drive further north to a beach just north of Townsville, pukka little spot, great beach with a view of Magnetic Island. It's a shame the area is flooded with Crocs, because it looks like a lovely place to have a swim. Looking forward to getting the ferry over to Magnetic Island in the morning and spending a few days there. Just to let ya know, we have drove just under 3000 kilometers already and we aint even half way.

Well the thought of Maggy Island was nice until we found out it cost $180 just to get the car on the ferry, fuck that for a laugh. So we ventured further north and decided to take the scenic route to Cairns and found a sweet spot by the huge lake in the middle of a rainforest to set up camp for the night. All over Oz you see signs to be careful of Kangaroo's whilst driving, but recently since we have entered the tropics we have seen signs to be careful of Cassowary's. They are like a mutated offspring of a T-Rex and a Turkey. Unfortunately still yet to see one. The next morning we took a drive to Cairns, which is one of the most breathtaking drives I've done. Its curvy roads went up and over the Rainforest Mountains to reveal all of northern Queensland east coast beaches.

Once we got to Cairns we noticed there were no rest areas for campervans or camper cars, so we treated ourselves to a hostel for the week. Plus Scott's birthday is coming up so it was good for the birthday boy to have a bed to bring some fat chick back to instead of a car. We bumped into a friend me and Scotty used to work with on the west coast (Maggy River), picking grapes. As well as some other dude I used to work with in Nomadz in Cairns. We went out every night in Cairns, some of which were definitely for the journal. Like the night we went to meet some old friends from Byron (Swedish Julia and French Violin player Antoine). We started off having a pre drink in Antoine's hostel 'Jack and Jillian's', and as we were playing a few drinking games in popped the entertainment staff from the bar downstairs and asked us if we wanted to win some free drink. All we had to do was get up on stage in an air sex competition, you basically have to do different sex positions on your own, shagging nothing but air. So 'challenge accepted' I got changed into a chicks dress and got up on stage with 7 other blokes who were just in their normal clothes, we had to pick a song and 1 by 1 get up in front of hundreds of people. Guess what, I only bloody won, happy days. Apart from making myself look like a complete prat in front of hundreds of people, it was an epic night.

The next day me, Scott, Krista and Brad drove to the crystal cascade waterfalls and spent the day swimming in the lagoon at the bottom. We told Sam from Maggy River about it when we got back and he was gutted he missed it. So we went back the next day with him and three other randoms for a BBQ, cliff jumping and more swimming. On the day of Scott's Birthday we all went to Cairns fake beach, the lagoon, and bumped into some girl from America I met on the east coast last year, Rachael. All these old friends are popping up from all over the place. It was then we decided what to do for Scott's birthday. We booked a boat trip that took us out onto Fitzroy Island on the Barrier Reef, which had some special DJ playing, but special for Aussie DJ's is two bob for anyone else, nevertheless an awesome night. The boat had a bar on it, which was a touch because it took a good hour, and the Island was sick. We had a dinner round massive tables getting to know everyone, then the drinking games started on the dance floor. There was one game that a girl had to go up and out your shorts 5 times holding a chewing gum, then chew it and blow a bubble. I had no hope, I was wearing the tightest jean shorts and once the girl finally got her hand up resting on my nob, she couldn't pull it back out, I'm not gonna lie I did not mind losing that game. When we got back to Cairns, we had VIP treatment in all the clubs, happy days, epic night.

Me and Scott left Cairns a few days later and drove further north to go and stay with an old Kavos buddy 'Huwey'. It was great to see him as it's been like four years, we all had a lot to say over many spliffs. He had an awesome little set up. His tent was in a campground outside a hostel, it was hilarious, he had the biggest tent there, thought he was a right little pimp. We left Port Douglas and decided to drive back down south and head for Darwin. It's a shame because Darwin is further north than Cairns, but the lazy Aussies could only be bothered to build a few roads, so we had to come back down, across and back up. Before we left the rainforest we decided to spend the day and night at a different canyon with waterfalls, for me these falls were my favourite for Cairns. We then started the bush to outback road trip, which I must say is boring as hell especially now all the weeds gone. I've literally been keeping myself busy, guessing what type of road kill we pass, so far it's been kangaroo's, cows, pigs, rabbits and foxes. No wonder all the birds in Oz are massive, there's a roadside buffet with fresh meat every morning. We are camped up at a rest area just outside Mt Isa, on the edge of Queensland, ready to enter the outback of the Northern Territory. The view of the stars here are speechless, I haven't words to describe it other than shit hot.

Shapnin me old Mukka, fuck it's been a mental couple of weeks. Our car finally made it to Darwin, thank fuck. Fair play to Scott, he drove the whole 7000 kilometers. Let me tell ya, road trips always seem fun until you're away from beaches and rainforests, and all there is to look at is desert, stranded aboriginals, and dead Kangaroo's. When we first started the trip, we had a shit load of weed and had high hopes of meeting a couple of European backpackers heading our way. However the weed ran out within a week, and all we see were retired Aussie couples.

Once we got to Darwin we met some welsh dude (Elliot) and his English missus, and he told us a good place to park and sleep, by the beach, with showers and power points. So we took their advice and stayed there a few nights. It was all fun and games until one morning the old bill woke us up, and give us $140 fine each for sleeping in public places.

I got in touch with an old Kavos buddy Stuart, who now lives in Darwin with his missus, and he let us stay at his gaff for a week until we flew to Bali. His gaff is the nuts, air-con in every room, swimming pool in the garden, opposite a golf course. They live with another couple from England, and they are moving out roughly the same time we get back, so there will be two spare bedrooms in this three bedroom palace, for when we get back from Bali, happy fucking days. I fucking love Darwin, the weather never drops below 30 all year round, the wages are shit hot and the night life is awesome. We met up with scouse Adam and his Irish missus who we used to work with in Gatton and went out on the piss with them, wicked night.

Once we applied for our Tax Back and got drunk with Stuart for a week, we boarded our flight to Bali. We met two girls on the flight and again at our hostel in Bali Dorian (French), and Dillan (Belgium). Once we put our bags in the 15 bed dorm, which had triple bunk beds. We all went for dinner and decided to get a room together, as it's cheaper and might both get laid from it. So the next day we found a place with four beds closer to Kuta nightlife and beach. That night we all went out to a bar called Beanstalk for a free hour of drinking from 8-9pm. Definitely drunk my own body weight in cocktails. It was a pukka bar, it had 8 floors, with fire shows and all sorts of weird shit going on, full of Aussie and European sex on legs, sick night. The next morning we had breakfast together and decided to get a cab to the east coast to get a boat to the Gili Islands. But as you do in south East Asia, get stitched up like a kipper and ended up getting not a speed boat but a fucking ferry to Lombok. It's not the end of the world because we was going to Lombok after Gili Trawangan, to climb a volcano and I would personally rather climb a volcano then sit on a beach. It's funny how things change I was planning to spend a week in Kuta surfing and getting drunk for free in Beanstalk, and one smell of French/Belgium GETS and I'm getting a boat to go volcano trekking, oh well.

Oh my days me best booky old pal, volcano trekking is one of the best things I've ever done. We all spent two days on the beach of Sengigi on Lombok before the trek. Which was a lot of fun, apart from the fact is that it's Ramadan at the moment, and Lombok is a Muslim Island. So all over the place there have been these mad and very loud, preaches and prayers coming out of speakers. Luckily for us our apartments were right next to a mosque with speakers I think set up by the ministry of sound. Indonesia is mad, it has so many different religions and languages. I think spread out over 2000 Islands of Indonesia, there are over 300 languages, so I've given up trying to learn some of the lingo. We had to wake up at 5am to get our taxi to the foot of Mt Rinjani to start our trek. We had breakfast and met the rest of our group. It's Me, Scott, Dorian, Dillan, Chris and Tom (Swiss dudes), and Nick (Aussie Guy). Plus our tour guide and his four porters, who are going to carry all our camping equipment, water and food.

We climbed for four hours, stop for lunch and then climbed another three hours to a place where we set up camp, on the rim of the volcano's crater. It's the most breathtaking sight I've ever seen. The crater had some huge lake in the middle, with another small looking volcano coming out of its lake. This small looking volcano was the remainders of molten lava in the 2004 eruption. The whole rim of the crater is well above the clouds as we are now at an altitude of 8000 feet. The walk up to this camp was fucking hard, but entertaining at the same time, as there are hundreds of monkeys all over the mountain. We watched the most beautiful sunset from above the clouds. The view was fucking mad, behind me was the crater of this natural monster, and in front of me was the sun setting right over the top of Bali's volcano. Fuck me book it didn't take long for my feelings to change, because as soon as that sun fucked off, it was freezing. So really good first day, but screwed over by a shit night's sleep.

We woke up bright and early for breakfast, then started day two by climbing down into the crater for a swim in the lake. After a freezing cold swim, we ventured on past a huge waterfall, into a spot where there were natural hot springs. These natural hot baths were heated by the gases creeping through the cracks in the mountain boiled from the lava below. It was the first hot bath I've had since England, went down like a treat. After lunch by the springs we carried on climbing up and out over the crater towards Mt Rinjani's summit. The peak of its summit is 3752 meters from sea level, which we were told on the way up we might not reach, because of the dangerously strong winds we were having. I thought the winds were abit much last night, when our tent nearly took off. We reached our camp in time for another sunset, and the stars from up here, pisses all over the stars you see in the outback, seriously felt like I was in space.

The next morning we woke up at 2am, so we could try and make the climb to the summit for sunrise. This day has got to be the toughest and scariest day of my life. Me and the boys left our guide with the girls behind half way up, as it was too dangerous for the girls to continue. The climb took three and a half hours in below freezing temperatures, with winds so strong you had to be on all fours and crawl up it. It got to a point where I thought I was going to die. The path got so narrow you had to go single file, with a cliff edge both sides, my hands turned blue and I was struggling to breathe. It was pitch black, so I didn't know who was in front or who was behind, so I just kept my head down and just kept crawling as turning back was definitely more dangerous than heading on. Luckily I found Scott cuddled up by some rocks, we tried having a spoon for body heat, but was doing us no favours, so we just kept going, and with only ten minutes before sunrise we made it to the top, being re-united with the boys. The euphoric moment we had standing on the top in perfect time for sunrise, is something I will remember forever. I'm usually a bit of a bitch when it comes to pushing myself beyond my limits, but this day was a proud moment for me. It was only us five at the top, we were looking down on all the people we passed on the way up, what a fucking rush.

Again the moment didn't last too long, as I had not one ounce of energy left and had to get off this fucking volcano. It took us a further seven hours to get back to where we got picked up. Fuck me, I was in bits. The total walk for the three day trek was 31 kilometers. That's right 31k up and down sharp molten lava and slippery volcanic ash. It's one of those LML/FML moments. Once we made it down alive, we took a taxi for an hour to the west coast of Lombok to get a boat to Gili Trawangan. It was mad, in the morning I was looking down at this Island from the summit, and now staring up at its peak above the clouds on a beautiful beach. Already loving the Gili's, they say it's an Asian Ibiza, so yes we have been out every night so far. We have been meeting up with the rest of the crew from the trek, as everyone went to the Gili's after Lombok. The mushy shakes here are very weak compared to Thailand, nevertheless been drinking them by the pint. Really do love it here, there are no cars or motorbikes, just bicycles and horse and cart. The food and drink is really good and cheap, plus there are GETS everywhere. Today me, Scott and the girls hired out a glass bottom boat and went snorkeling around the three Gili Islands. We got to see a shit load of turtles and tropical fish, wicked day. Now just chilling in the room having a few joints before we start getting ready for Dorian's last night, as much as she's been a cock block I'm going to miss Frenchy.

Booky boy I only bloody made it through the Gili's alive, fuck me what a wicked couple of weeks it was. The morning after Dorian left, me and Dillan went and found another place to stay, Scott was meant to come but had 1 to many mushy shakes and didn't get up. So he had to move again the following night. When we first went out with the Swiss, they wasn't to keen on doing mushys, now they do more than us, they love it, bless em. As its Ramadan the only place to go out past 11pm was a silent disco in some Irish bar, but one night we took a walk and found a bar on the beach playing music till 7am, with fire shows and dance comps. Happy fucking days, the only problem was not many people knew about this bar, so every night after the silent disco, me, Scotty and the Mt Rinjani trekkers would promote the after party and got it pumping.

I've been loving the daytimes here just as much. Me and Scott take our snorkels north of the Island and just float back to the south, as there is a perfect rip tide that brings you back. It was like being back on the Barrier Reef, some seriously funky looking marine life out there. One by one all the friends we have made on this island were leaving, and it started to feel like Christmas on Koh Phangan all over again, we felt like locals. So after a really messy night that left me and Scott bed-bound for two days, we decided to leave Gili T, and get back to Bali. I think the final straw for me was waking up to some old Aussie chick leaving my room, like the scene from the movie Inbetweeners, 'kitty don't bite, not now she's been fed', errr still sends me shivers. After the roughest boat trip back to Bali, we arrived at our new destination, 'Ubud'. We was going to have a detox, but a couple of German GETS we bumped into on the Gili's wanna get drunk with us tonight, so yes an absolute 'getting Dogs#!t' is in order tonight.

What's crackalackin booky boy, we are finally back in Australia, thank fuck. It was a great 4 weeks holiday in Indonesia, but was not good for my health. After a night of salsa dancing with the Germans in Ubud, we spent the day in monkey forest. It's an old ancient forest with religious ruins buried deep within, covered with monkeys. Some of them can be right nasty little bastards, I wasn't really a fan of any of the gits, until I see one climb up on this Aussie dudes head and take a piss. We was going to book up some white water rafting, but the weather was a bit shabby and because of the dry season, we was told the rapids were not that extreme. So we fucked it off and decided to go back to the south of Bali, where the accommodation and booze is cheap, with plenty of GETS to go around.

We got a taxi to Seminyak, which is about 5k north of Kuta. The nightlife here was crap, but the shopping was spot on, as well as the best Indian curry I've had in a long time. We treated ourselves to another massage probably number five of the holiday, and got our ears sucked dry with wax candles. You should have seen the amount of shit that came out of my ears, not a pretty sight. The next day we got a taxi down to Kuta to spend our last 6 days getting rat assed for free in Beanstalk. It was a mental last week, we spent our days down the beach watching some mean ass waves kicking the shit out of some surfers who couldn't surf to save their life, or just chilled by the pool in our half decent resort. By night we would go to Beanstalk and get as much free piss as we could before hitting all the other bars.

Me and Scotty were so disappointed by the shabby mushys on Gili T, we promised ourselves no more. However one night, we came across one of the hundred mushy stalls and asked the guy if we could pick our own mushys, so we did and helped ourselves to all the best ones, and fuck me did we get high. Apart from the run-down beach, stinky roads and the constant hassle from locals selling shit on the street, Kuta is a great laugh. We met some really cool people, a number of amazing Gets and had some wicked nights out. Although Indonesia will be missed, I was relieved to be back on Aussie soil.

Only been back a week and already feel 100 times better, it's a great feeling having a solid poo again. We spent our first week job searching and luckily Me and Scotty got ourselves a job starting Monday. So to celebrate Me, Scott, Stuart and Nathan all done a bar crawl on Friday night. It was more of a leaving do for Nathan as he and his missus were leaving the next day. Which was a good thing because me and Scott are sharing a bedroom and once they fuck off we get a room each. It was such a funny night. We started off in a strip club, then headed off into many other bars before ending up in a gay nightclub. It was meant to be a gay bar, but just full of straight Gets, happy days. We bumped into a few old faces that night, scouse Adam and his missus from our Gatton farming days, Hayden my mate from Byron Bay and some Scottish chick Wee Jen an old friend from Kavos. It's been a good weekend, after Friday night we had a send-off BBQ on Saturday for the guys, watched a mad bush fire next to our house on Saturday night, and Sunday we spent all day in the pool waiting for our roast dinner to be cooked. Really looking forward to starting work tomorrow, so I can start saving instead of spending.

Ahh hello booky wooky, I've well neglected you this past month, but let me tell ya, it's been a goodun. Mine and Scotty's job is going well, we are testing soils and concretes in a laboratory, as weird as it sounds it sweet as a nut. We are in shade thank fuck, because Darwin doesn't drop below 30 degrees day and night, as well as the humidity always over 80%, it's a good job we are inside. Plus it's a 5 minute drive and the moneys pretty good, so happy fucking days. We are working 6 days a week, but do half day Saturdays, so still get a half decent weekend. We've had some bloody gooduns as well. A few weeks back we took a drive to Crocodilus Park, it's basically half crocodile farm, half zoo. The croc part was sick, they had some crocs bigger than 6 meters, we got to feed the big ones and hold the babies, it was wicked. The zoo was the nuts as well, they had Lions, Tigers, Cassowary's, all kinds of Monkeys and Snakes, the list goes on. Stuart had been before and remembered you could play hide and seek with the Lioness, it was wicked. You could tell she so wanted to bite his head off after 10 minutes of making her run up and down the side of her huge cage in the heat, bless her.

That night me and Scott went out in the city, good old Mitchell Street, we had a little re-union again. Anna and Matilda, the Swedish girls we know from the east coast were in Darwin for a week, so we met up with them as well as Hayden and his mates and got proper 'Dogs#!t'. The next day we all took a drive to Berry Springs, it's about an hour's drive to a national park, with these pukka little fresh water swimming holes. It was lovely, beer, BBQ, sun, swimming with buddies I've met from around the world, one of them Sagapo my life moments. I bloody miss Matty boy, he's doing ok though, back in Byron Bay, Getting ready for summer. Him and Caz are still going strong, looks like he's got his visa sorted, the lucky fucker. Ah good luck to him, can't wait to see him, I'm thinking about surprising him in a few month's time on his birthday for a little sneaky weekend away to Byron.

Unfortunately it looks like my time in Oz is coming to an end, if I want to stay, I need to do it through a sponsorship visa, which is easy to get up here in Darwin, it's just that it's a 4 year commitment, which I have not got in me. Fuck me, I don't stay in a place longer than 4 months, let alone 4 years. Especially Darwin, it's too hot for Aboriginals up here, so gingers have got no hope. So I'm going to save up until Christmas and travel round Asia for 4 months, to hopefully give England a little time to warm up before returning back. Just to let you know my good old bible of justice, I bought myself a guitar, I'm going to try and learn in time for my brother Matt's wedding next April in Cyprus. God help me, her name is Doris, and we know 2 chords, which is fucking pathetic, so I'm gonna have to love ya and leave ya, me and old Doris are gonna get our jam on.

Fuckinnnelllll book, where you been all my life, it's been well over a month, and life is fucking sweet at the moment. The soil testing business is going strong, but not saving as much as I would like to, due to mainly the fact that we are drinking a lot. All day in work I drink about 4 liters of water, so once I get home, water is the last thing I want, and because of the heat the only thing I find hydrating is beer. Since I've been back from Bali I've been talking to Bolly, who's been down in Melbourne working, her plan was to visit me in Darwin for a week, before she started her travels round Asia.

Well the week of her visit has come and gone, and it was amazing. I truly love her with all my heart and the feeling is mutual. So instead of going Asia she decided to hang about until I've saved enough, so we can go together, she got herself a job delivering horses across Australia, which is going to last roughly 6 weeks, which is handy because we have got just under 2 months before we fly to Asia. Since she's been gone we have stayed in contact, by phone every day and our love is growing by every phone call. I'm really pining over nana Bolly, hence my new nickname which Bird gave me (ginger pine cone). A good friend of mine, scouse Nicky (who you may remember from Perth) arrived in Darwin a few weeks ago. She come and stay at the house for a few weeks until she started her job in a roadhouse a few hours south of here. Its funny because Me, Scott, Stuart and Nicky all have got the same tattoo, we got done in Kavos in 2008. It's a re-union dated 10 years from the day we got it done, we have to meet under the Eiffel tower in Paris at 12.00 midday. It's just so random that out of the 10 people who got it done, 4 of us are in Darwin.

We had a pukka weekend just gone, we went camping in Litchfield National Park again, fucking love that place, it's a beautiful place to go with a group of friends and get 'Dogs#!t'. Just thought I would let you know Mr. Bible, Bolly fucked that job off, as she was being treated like a mug, so she is on her way back to Darwin, wooooooo, I can't wait to see her, I'm picking her up from the airport tonight, I'm so happy right now, fucking love Bolly, and Fucking love you book.

Well, well, well, if it isn't my best buddy in the world, where the fuck have you been all my life. I'm getting proper shit at keeping up to date with you. Another month or so has passed, and the excitement is building for Asia, only got 4 weeks till we fly, cant fucking wait. As much as I hate soil testing and Darwin's climate, I'm gonna miss this place especially Stuey and Bird, fucking love them two stumblebums. Me and Bolly are doing really well, love her to bits, I'm so happy she is back in my life. She has got herself two jobs, working in 'Rush' the surf shop, as well as cleaning properties under Bird's management, so she is happy to earn back the money she lost doing the stupid outback horse thing.

The wet season has pretty much arrived, we have seen some pukka storms, can't wait to see a cyclone, fingers crossed there's not one on the 17th December, when we fly. We have a new recruit to the animal house, Yogi the kitten, unfortunately Indi fucked off and hasn't returned, which really upset Bird, as Indi was the first, so Yogi is the replacement. Yogi and Bella the other kitten are doing really well, as soon as Yogi grows his dick big enough, he is blatantly going to fuck Bella, it's on the cards, bless em. I haven't saved the money I was hoping to save, so will not last as long as I wanted in Asia before returning home. I'm not bothered though because the more I think about England, the more I want to be there. I miss all the Hawkins so fucking much, luckily for me I will be home in time for my brother Matty's stag do, cant fucking wait.

Booksta you little slag 'Bo, how the fuck are ya. I'm fucking tip top, thanks for asking, it's December and Christmas couldn't come any sooner. Can't believe I've only got two weeks left in Oz, I'm missing it already and I'm still here. I've had a pukka couple of weeks since we last spoke, Bolly's birthday was a goodun. We had a fajita and vodka jelly shot night, everyone had work the next day so we didn't go out, but still we all managed to get pretty 'Dogs#!t'. Me and Bolly have been getting some alone time in this mad house. We got up for a sunrise over Elizabeth bridge and been down to Mindle beach for a sunset, I love Darwin you get the best of both worlds for sunsets and rises. We also went to the bridge for an awesome lightning storm, got completely wet through, but was well worth it.

The weekend just gone was a goodun, didn't go to work on Saturday, as we all got horseshit Friday night, so I went with Bolly to watch her do her skydive. She fucking loved it, gutted I couldn't do it with her, but funds are tight. After her dive we packed the car with all our camping equipment, then drove to Litchfield national park. We got to Burley rock pools in time for a dip and a beer in the natural springs before cooking our dinner on our campfire for sunset. It was a really good day all in all, I'm so glad Bolly enjoyed her birthday week. After dinner we had a couple of beers and a few joints, whilst playing cards, but had to call it a night because we come so unprepared with lights and torches and it was getting dark, plus Bolly started itching out thinking she had something on her, so we crawled into our tent after the fire went out. It ended up that Bolly was right about the creepy crawlies, because in the morning she woke up to a cockroach on her, which she had felt all night. So we got out of our tent sharpish, packed up our shit and went for a morning swim in the rock pools. Then we drove to Wangi falls and spent the day there, swimming and forest trekking. Once we got out of the waterfall, the park ranger had told people not to go in, as there were fresh and salt water crocs roaming about, so we were fucking lucky really. On our way home we stopped at Berry Springs for a BBQ breakfast, which was a lovely little treat to end a pukka weekend.

Just to let ya know Booky wooky, we have booked a flight from India to Amsterdam for the 28th march, so we have a rough plan on how long we have got, till we can get high before returning home. I've got to go Bolly keeps trying on clothes and its turning me on, see ya soon best book for a buddy.

Journal 3

Shapnin book, so here we are book number 3. Just to let you know, you are a present from my gorgeous girlfriend Bolly. Well fuck me book of justice I'm only in bloody Thailand again, can't get enough of this place. Me and my Aussie adventures have come to an end, it's been a mad couple of years and I've loved every minute of it. I'm going to miss Australia so much, especially the end of my trip in Darwin. Stuart and Bird have been so good to us, giving us a place to live and a car to drive once we sold Sebastian the Subaru, I cannot thank them enough, for helping us get settled and to start saving, after coming back from Bali skint.

Our last few weeks in Oz were pukka, we had ourselves a fake Christmas, just so we could celebrate with the guys before we left. It was a wicked day. Stuarts brother was there to join us (who I think is an absolute cunt), but that's another story, as well as scouse Nicky who returned from her work in the outback. All seven of us done secret Santa and had to buy each other presents to wear on Christmas day, (well the 15th December, our fake Christmas). Stuart got me a wonder woman outfit, Bolly got Stuart a French maids outfit, Scott got Bolly a clowns outfit, Bird got Scott a French maids outfit, Stu's brother got Bird a nun's outfit, Nicky got Stu's bro a Disney wand, lipstick and pink shoes, and I got Nicky a hippy wig with matching ballerina shoes. Proper random shit I know but was a funny start to an awesome day. Now I know I have told you how hot

Darwin is, so you can imagine we didn't keep our costumes on for long, but once we got drunk they come back on soon enough. We had a BBQ lamb roast, which went down a treat, followed by six bottles of random spirits and three cartons of piss, (cases of beer in English). It was a messy night, full of drinking games in the pool.

Unfortunately the next day we had to pack and get ready for our flight the following day. Me, Bolly and Scott were now ready to get out of Darwin and enjoy Asia once again. We said our goodbyes to Stuart, Bird, Nicky and the dickhead of a sibling Stuart calls bro, and boarded our flight to Bali, to get a connecting flight to Kuala Lumpur. Luckily we booked a few nights accommodation in Reggae Mansion hostel in KL, because we arrived at 1am. So glad we booked this place, because it was the nuts, best hostel I've stayed in, pisses all over the Aussie hostels. It had these cool little booths for beds, instead of bunk beds, its own cinema room, a bar and restaurant on the bottom floor, which was proper plush, and a bar on the rooftop looking over the city.

After a good night's sleep in our comfy prison cells, we got a train north of the city to some sacred caves in the mountains, 'Batu Caves'. These caves were awesome, it took over 300 stairs to climb up to it, which were infested with monkeys. At the top were a loads of sacred shrines, statues and temples, as well as another dark cave we had to pay for to get into. This cave smashed it, it had many different types of bats and insects, which eco system have all survived off of bats poo for thousands of centuries. Inside this cave had a rare spider only ever to be found in this specific cave, as well as poisonous snakes and centipedes, scary as fuck, but great fun. We got back to China town, which is where our hostel was and treated ourselves to a Nando's, then got back to Reggae Mansion and started to get on it, on the rooftop with the other backpackers we have met. We had a good drink ending up in a bar down the road which funny enough was called Reggae bar.

The next day we had a good walk round the city, seeing the PETRONAS towers which are an amazing set of buildings. Before coming to Kuala Lumpur I had visions of it being like Bangkok, polluted, full of temples and slums. However this city was far from that, it was just as developed as London, and as much as I would have preferred it to be 3rd world and different to a western city, was nice to see a developing Asia. We left the city after Scott got kicked out of an outdoor swimming pool for not seeing the sign 'under 12's only' and got back to our hostel to watch a movie in our private cinema. We had dinner and behaved ourselves that night because we had a flight to catch to Koh Samui the next day. This flight was the bollox, I loved it, it only held about 100 people and had propellers to start it. Bolly and Scott hated it as they don't like flying, but for me, it felt like I was doing another skydive, definitely flying with that airline again.

We arrived in Samui and got a taxi to Lamai, we sat down in a bar while Bolly had a look round the town for some accommodation. She is a legend, she found us a perfect room on the beach with air-con, fridge, TV, double and a single bed for 4 four quid a night, could not have asked for better, she's definitely the room hunter from now on. We done exactly what we wanted to do that night, have a fat curry followed by a massage and a smoke, perfect first night in Thailand. The next day we rented out some bikes, and drove inland to see some temples and get blessed by a monk. Then drove to the foot of a waterfall and climbed to the top. There was a path by the side of the waterfall to get to the top, but I do love a challenge, so we done some rock climbing right up through the center of it, fucking love a good trek. We drove back to Lamai, and had dinner in some proper shit box restaurant which had pukka tasting food, all for about a quid, then went back and started getting ready to go out in the town north of Lamai 'Chewang'. We got to Chewang expecting to get on the mushys, but we couldn't find anyone selling them, so decided to go to the

Ice bar, which was fucking sick. They give us big fur coats, Russian hats and wooly gloves, the bar was -7 degrees and everything was made from Ice, even the glasses you drank out of. It was a pukka bar, outside in the smoking area it had a beer pong table and a magician walking round doing some proper shabby tricks. After the Ice bar we got back to Lamai to watch a fire show on the beach.

It wasn't really a messy night, which I'm glad of, because we rented more bikes out the next day to do some more waterfall trekking. As we drove half way up this waterfall we noticed a restaurant/bar that had a swimming pool with an infinite edge that looked over the island. It was beautiful, so instead of more trekking we decided to chill out here for the day. We got back from Lamai in time to meet a friend of ours from England, 'Josh' and for Bolly to get her new tattoo. We had an early one the night to catch our boat the next day to Koh Phangan. Josh had only just arrived in Samui, so unfortunately had to say goodbye until he was going to join us on Phangan for Christmas.

Luckily for us, my Norwegian friends Kaia and Eline had reserved us a few rooms, which was well needed as 'Had Rin Beach' gets very busy in peak season. It was so good to see the girls as well as an old Byron Bay buddy Swedish Dan. That day we arrived, me and Bolly went to mushroom mountain, while Scott went out with the rest and got on it. Bless him he was gagging to go out and have sex with some random backpacker, and success it was, he pulled himself some dirty get from Holland who was half Israel'y, called Tequila. Me and Bolly had a wicked trip in mushy mountain, followed by weirdo watching on the beach. The next day was Christmas Eve, which for the Scandinavians was Christmas day. So we all spent the day on the beach, playing drinking games like, 'Beersfree'. Which is a game of Frisbee with beer funny enough. That night we went for dinner, then onto a bar full of Scandinavians singing weird Christmas songs, funny old breed, the Vikings, you gotta love em. We decided to go back to rooms to play more drinking games and sing more weird Christmas songs, singing and dancing around our decorated Christmas tree. Love the rooms we are staying in, every room has a balcony, and everyone staying in all the rooms in our half shabby.com resort, know each other in one way or another through travelling. We had a half sensible Christmas eve, because we didn't want to ruin the real Christmas on the 25th.

Yay its Christmas, me and Bolly woke up and opened our presents. I got a sweet ass Pandora bracelet, and family guy Christmas t-shirt, Bolly got a few necklaces from me, as well as many cards and presents sent from her family back in England. It was a lovely morning, I fucking love that girl, she's definitely a keeper. We all went to a traditional English pub that afternoon and had a traditional English roast, with all the trimmings, absolutely cream in your pants sort of munch. There were a shit load of us, all in absolute heaven seeing Yorkshire puds and Guinness on draught. We got back to Had Rin and raved it up once again on the beach.

The next day struggling as we were, finally started sunbaving, need a tan. Scotty bless him don't learn his lesson and got ill from getting on it too much, so now he's on antibiotics and can't drink for five days. Me and Bolly had a couple of days off as well to save some money and get a tan. Well tell a lie, not completely off, because one day we fancied doing some daytime mushys. Tripping out in the daytime is weird but equally as good. So after a refreshing week, the 28th of December full moon party popped up all of a sudden and Had Rin was packed. So as you do on a full moon, we got dressed up in florescent shit and covered in florescent paint and got absolutely 'Dogs#!t'. Surprise surprise, I was in bed first, thanks to Bolly putting me to bed bless her, but I'm glad she went out and enjoyed her night until sunrise. Josh turned up for the full moon party, but unfortunately he got deeply horseshit and lost his wallet, so only after being here only one day he wanted to leave because he hated Phangan, fucking faggot.

The next day was just another day of sunbaving and a lot of people feeling sorry for themselves. The majority of us had an early one that night because the next day we was planning to rent out a few jeeps and do a tour of the island. However not everyone behaved themselves that night, so we decided not to rent cars, but to pay some Thai dude to drive us around all day in his tuk tuk taxi, which is basically an open back truck with some shabby roof. It was a great day, we went to a lake which had a rope swing, from the bar into the lake, and visited a pukka beach which was a lot better than Had Rin. We got there at a good time as well, because the tide was at a perfect time to leave a walkway to the island. This derelict island was nothing apart from a few bamboo made huts and what looked like a bar, which seemed like they got destroyed in a storm. Unfortunately we couldn't stay at this place too long, because our friend was in a bikini competition back in Had Rin and needed as much support as possible because there was a lot of money up for grabs.

On the way back to Had Rin, we stopped off at a resort where a friend of mine was staying I know from England, 'Blacky'. I grew up with this dude and have not seen him in over two years. We picked up Blacky and his missus, 'Eva', and got back to Had Rin in time for the bikini competition. We was going to behave ourselves that night, because the next day was new years eve, but got excited seeing Blacky, so decided to go out. We all went for dinner in some shit box restaurant, with great tasting food and whilst eating, the whole island had a power cut, kinnnneeellllll. It wasn't a massive problem because we bought some candles to have a shower and get ready after dinner. Still wanting to have a sensible night, we decided to have a mushroom night. It was a goodun, Blacky and his missus didn't do mushys but me, Bolly, Scott and some English chick Holly all got high. That night we bumped into some chick from my hometown, Lucy and a scouse dude we met in Australia, Adam from Gatton and Darwin. It was a good night, it was lovely to catch up with Blackatack after so long. That night it started raining and hasn't stopped since, its now new years eve and doesn't look like it's going to be the greatest night as everywhere is flooded, but still, it is NYE and getting 'Dogs#!t' is on the cards no matter what the weather, so fuck it. Mr. Book of awesome memories, I shall wish you a happy new year, and I will see you in 2013, let the 'Dogs#!t' commence.

Wooooooo its 2013 baby, and what a great way to start a fresh year, had rin, Thailand. The count down to 12 o'clock was a bit disappointing, because there wasn't really a countdown, it just kinda went off. The fireworks were pukka, they got shot from a mountain in the direction of the beach and all fell right next to us in the sea. Not long after midnight we were all dancing about ten to twenty feet away from some dude getting shot by accident in the way of 2 Thai dudes. Its fucking scary knowing it could have been anyone of us. Once everyone had calmed down after the shooting me Scott and Bolly went to the mountain for a sneaky sunrise mushroom shake. Once the sun had come up, we walked back down to Smacktus bar to carry on dancing with the rest of the crew, but it started pissing down, so we decided to go back to the room. Me and Bolly sat on our balcony watching everyone come home one by one, it was hilarious, perfect entertainment for a couple still high on mushys, we ended up sitting there till midday. By the time we decided to hit the sack our balcony was full of people.

We woke up that afternoon and had to pack, as we was catching a boat out of here the next day. What a fucking horrible journey it was, we got a 2 hour boat ride back to mainland, said goodbye to the rest of the crew, as from here, we were going to Phuket while the rest went Phi Phi. We got on some shit tip of a bus at the port, drove about an hour to a place where we were going to change buses, but after being told to get off the bus, we were told to get back on it, and drove half hour down the road and told to get off it again. Travelling Thailand is hard work, they are so unorganised and no one has a clue what's going on. We waited at this place for about 3 hours, then finally got a bus that took 5 hours to get to Phuket. It didn't take us to long to find a room in Patong, Phuket, thank fuck because Scott had a violent a case of sickness and diarrhea. The only reason we are in Patong is to wait for Bolly's sister who gets here on the 4th. The sooner she gets here the better, because this place stinks, it's like a combination of Kavos and Armpit.

So Mr. Journal, how the hell are you? It's been to long me old mukka. There's not much to say about Phuket, it's always same old same old on this island, beaches are shit, far too many tourists and the night life is full of peado's and lady boys. Not a great fan of Patong, never have been. Whilst we were waiting for Montana (Bolly's sister) to arrive, we had a few little treats like some shopping, game of bowling and movie at the cinema, Hobbit, awesome film. We did get a tuk tuk to another beach down the road, 'Kata Beach', which was a good day out, but still far too many tourists for my liking. So after a few days of being sick, shitting razor blades and being bored and fed up of Russians. We finally meet Montana. The night she arrived we all went in search of a Ping Pong show. Unfortunately all that was on offer were 'Go Go Bars', and that's only fun when your single. So yea, thanks a bunch Bolly, ha-ha. So we ended up having a couple of beers and getting an early night, as we were getting a boat to Phi Phi the next morning.

Patong is not far from the port which is a touch as I fucking hate a full mini bus. We got to the boat early enough to find ourselves a plot on top deck, really miss my mum at the minute, this time last year we were doing the exact same trip together. The boat journey weren't too sad, it wasn't choppy at all and the sun was avin it. When we arrived on Phi Phi, it was a fucker to find a room, everywhere was fully booked. We managed to check in to a hostel, there were 2 rooms, me and the girls checked in to 1 room with 17 other guys and Scott checked in to a room with 19 other girls, so yeah you can imagine Scott's face when he went in to the room. Luckily for us, but not for Scott, we found a better room that was available the next day. The Aussie woman who owned it came to Thailand a year after the 2004 Tsunami to help with the devastation, found herself a little Thai husband feel in love, had 2 kids and built a complex with a bar, restaurant and places to stay from all old bits of timber from the wreckage from the Tsunami. It's the best looking place I've stayed in Thailand, proper old school rooms, literally on the beach, in my element.

Feel a bit sorry for Scott because he was in a room with 19 gets and now he's spending the week sharing a bed with Montana. Oh well, you win some you lose some. When we got to Phi Phi everyone from Phangan was already here, Blacky and Eva, the

Norwegians and the rest of the Christmas and New Year's Eve crew. It was a pukka week, Blacky and Eva was meant to leave the second day we got there to Koh Lanta but they ended up staying a few days extra and just done a day trip to Lanta, so we had a few leaving do's for them. We had a boat trip booked to see Phi Phi Ley, (The Beach), but Montana had one too many buckets the night before and could not handle the thought of a boat. We postponed it for the day after, when we eventually got on the boat the next day it was an awesome day out. We see some beautiful beaches, a shit load of monkeys and heaps of fishes while snorkeling. The trip ended with an amazing sunset from our long boat in the middle of the Andaman Sea.

It was mine and Bolly's 3 month anniversary on the 10th so we let Scott entertain Montana for the day while me and Bolly took a long boat to a random beach to the other side of the island. It was quite lucky how we come across this beach, because when we got in the long boat I didn't have a clue where we was going, but luckily when we drove round the island we spotted a pukka little beach, so we told the skipper to pull over and wait a few hours for us. On this beach was one restaurant/bar and a few very old bamboo huts, owned by one man who was blatantly Bob Marley's Thai cousin. This guy had signs on all the trees saying no Israelis. Instantly we feel in love with this dude, what a legend. As much as me and Nana would have loved to have stayed on this beach for the night we had to get back because it's my birthday tomorrow, and I've arranged with the guys to celebrate it tonight as we were leaving the following day.

We got back to our humble abode, got ready and started getting on it. Me and Scott met Blacky and Eva in some Irish pub for a pint of Magners Draft which went down a treat. Cheers Blacky good fucking shout. Then not long after Bolly and Montana joined us in Reggae bar to watch some tourists kick the shit out of each other in the kick boxing ring, can seriously never get bored of that bar. Then we moved on to Banana bar to meet the rest of the crew for a few sneaky games of beer pong. At this point there were shit loads of us, and banana bar aint exactly massive so after a few free buckets compliments on the house we all went down to the beach, it was actually quite a successful night for me as I made it out as late as everyone else.

The next day I woke up, fresher than predicted realising I'm 27 years old. So straight down to the bar I went, and didn't actually leave that bar until I couldn't remember how old I was. Just what the doctor ordered. I couldn't really get too 'Dogs#!t' as we were getting a boat to Koh Lanta in the morning. All in all had a lovely birthday, and got some pukka presents from everyone and spent all day sitting on my ass drinking Jack Daniels. The journey to Koh Lanta was pretty sweet, the sea was calm and we found a sweet place to stay by one of the touts on the boat on the way over. Which was a touch because again we had nothing booked. This place was perfect it was on the beach with everything we needed, for such a cheap price, happy days.

It was all a bit doom and gloom when we got to Lanta because both the girls got ill and Scott realised he had to cut his Thailand trip short to catch a cheap flight back to Australia. Bolly bless her caught a real bad throat infection, similar to Scott had in Koh Phanang and Montana had a high fever. Yay my favourite island and everyone's moody. Still though we made it as enjoyable as we could, we had a few treats on Lanta, a couple of massages at sunset, big bag of weed and a night on the mushys. Love Lanta. We booked a day trip to the waterfalls and the elephant trip. Which was cool it was the same one I did last year, but nevertheless, still had a goodun. Scott left Lanta to catch a flight from Krabi, and me and the girls got a boat back to Phuket, which was an interesting journey because we had to change boats at Phi Phi in the middle of the ocean. Bolly and Montana were giggling all the way to Phuket about our day at the waterfall at Lanta, because on the flyer it said we would see a snake show and all we see was a few boxes of dead snakes. The tour guide kept telling us that the snakes were very special, because they don't eat or drink just sleep all day, I suppose it's a nice way of saying there all dead.

Once we got to Phuket we decided we didn't want to go back to Patong, as it's a complete shit hole, so we got a taxi to the beach north of Patong called Kamala. It was perfect, it had a decent beach, nice cheap restaurants and was close to the airport, so Montana would catch her flight the next day. Me and Bolly had booked a bus to Bangkok the same day. It was a VIP bus that took 12 hours, very comfy journey, seats were like the seats you get in Business class on a flight. We arrived in Bangkok about 6 in the morning, got a taxi straight to Khoasan road and found an apartment straight away. We had to spend the weekend in Bangkok to wait for the Indian embassy to open, to get our Indian visas.

It was a lovely weekend, during the day we kept getting on random buses and boats around the city on a mission to get lost. Every time we had to get a taxi back as we fulfilled our mission to get lost. It was so good to see parts of the city I've never seen, away from any westerners, felt proper local. The Saturday night we went to a few Go-go bars and a ping pong show. The show was awesome the chicks were shooting ping pongs and darts out of their front bums, drawing pictures with pens up them, as well as a live sex show.

Once we applied for our visas we left our passports in Bangkok and booked a 12 hour bus north to Chaingmai, it wasn't that bad of a journey the bus was empty. So me and Bolly managed to get a few chairs each to spread out and get some kip. Well that was the plan, but the driver was a smoker so he stopped every hour, and for what he said was a toilet break, knowing full well he just wanted a fag. We arrived in Chaingmai at 7 o'clock and fuck me it was freezing. This is the first time I have been cold since climbing the volcano on Lombok. Don't get me wrong it didn't take long to warm up once the day got going. It's just that Northern Thailand has a high altitude, so of a night, the temperatures drop.

We got a tuk tuk from the bus depot to our guest house Chaingmai Inn. The shower was proper shabby and the beds were rock solid but it was very cheap and in a great location. The first day there, we had a long walk in and around the city, and straight away feel in love with Chaingmai. There are hardly any tourists and everything was so cheap. Just what the doctor ordered. We found a pukka little stall/kitchen to eat at by the side of a road. The food was amazing and the beer was so cheap, in my element. After kicking Bolly's ass at shithead we decided to call it a night. We woke up early to spend a day seeing a lot of temples, we got a tuk tuk to the first temple called Wot-u-mong, not only has it got the best name, but it is literally my favourite temple I have been to. The temple was built underground and had loads of little funky caves and tunnels leading to shrines and stone carvings of different Buddha's. The grounds surrounding the temple were huge, full of random wild chickens and dogs. It was such a peaceful place, with monks meditating everywhere. We took a walk down to a lake and bought some food to feed the fish, which were massive but we ended up giving most of the food to a load of pigeons on an island in the middle of this lake. We spent a few hours at Wot-u-mong and still had many more temples to see. So we got a tuk tuk to take us to see 5 more temples around Chaingmai, they were all lovely and very different from each other, but personally they are nothing on Wot-u-mong. We decided to go and eat at the same restaurant/road side shack that night, love that place.

We rented out some bicycles the next day, to see parts of the city we had missed. Also Bolly has a gut feeling she might not get Indian visa so we got her a few things set up, as a backup plan in case she doesn't. For work she managed to find a volunteers position at an orphanage and for her accommodation she found a cool little one bed place at some French guest house. As much as I didn't wanna go India without her I could see how happy she was with this back up plan, and knowing it was only a few months until we had to get the flight we booked from Delhi to Amsterdam. I know my ginger pine cone status would not have lasted long. We found an English pub that night and treated ourselves to some pub grub it went down a treat. The next day we got up bright and early to catch a 4 hour bus further north to a town called Pai. The journey to Pai was a road up and down mountains with roughly 760 bends/corners, fucking missions if you ask me, but was so worth it.

Pai is the best place I've been to in Thailand yet. I've really been kicking myself, knowing this is my 5th time in Thailand and first time I've been to the north. The town itself is in a valley surrounded by beautiful mountains filled with waterfalls, canyons and natural hot springs. We both again had fallen in love with this new town. It was so hippy. I can't explain how laid back and happy the locals are here. We stayed in a bamboo bungalow across a river which you had to get there over a bamboo bridge that looks like it was made in the 1700's. Of a night this town come to life, no mad parties or drunken assholes, just a beautiful market with loads of hippy clothes and great food on the go. On the bus ride up here we met a couple of Canadian GETS and they advised us to rent out a motor bike to see the surrounding areas. So we rented a bike for a few days to see some shit.

The first day we drove to the natural hot springs, there were many pools which had signs to tell you how hot the temperature was, at the top, the pool was 80 degrees, which obviously was too hot bath in, however it had many people sitting by it boiling eggs, it was jokes, I mean I love a good picnic, and if I knew we could boil eggs here I would of bought a saucepan and a frying pan and had a good old full English. Luckily further, down had cooler pools to actually bath in at 37 degrees, sounds hot but nowhere near as hot as the hot springs on Mt Rinjani volcano on Lombok. After chilling there for a while we drove across a memorial ww2 bridge to 'Pai's canyon', which was amazing. We met a bunch of English dudes and trekked around the canyon with them for a while, until me and Bolly decided it would be a great place from here to watch the sunset. Therefore knowing how much temperatures drop of a night, we road back, had a shower and rapped up as warm as we could, bearing in mind our backpacks are full of Australian summer clothes. We got to the canyon in time for the most beautiful sunset over the northern Thai mountains. We got back to Pai after a dark cold journey, and enjoyed its scrumptious night market once again. That night we bumped into some Canadian chick and some English dude who were both separately in Pai on a break from work in Bangkok teaching English. They invited us back to their hostel which we had heard was a good crack through the grapevine, but after seeing the sunset, we thought it would be a great idea to have an early one and watch the sunrise, and just meet the guys the following night.

I woke up at 6 o clock when the alarm went off, Bolly was too cold, tired, and just plain lazy to get up, so I wrapped up in every layer possible and drove there on my own. Yes that's right a romantic, depressant of a man watching a sunrise on his own, thanks Bolly, thanks a bunch, to be perfectly honest couldn't give a fuck. It was amazing, as it was a full moon that sat over the mountain whilst in perfect symmetry the sun rose up from the rice paddies, as if it was a mirror, fucking Sagapo my life moment, for sure. I got back to show Bolly the pics but moany bollox as she is at the moment, couldn't care less. Once jabba crawled out of her hut, we had another exciting day ahead. We drove to a waterfall, which you could literally slide down because of the smooth rocks, and chilled there for a good few hours, loads of fun. There were a squadron of Thai army dudes all getting pissed up and throwing each other down it. Don't get me wrong it wasn't safe and people got hurt, but was jokes to watch. We ended up bumping into the same guys we did at the canyon the day before, as well as a few more from their hostel, and spent an hour or 2 at some traditional Chinese village, it was weird, it felt like we was in China, although I've never been, but still obviously in Thailand. Bolly treated herself to a donkey ride, whilst me and a few other dudes, enjoyed this traditional Chinese swing, hours of fun, well twenty minutes, good while it lasted. We got back to Pai in time to have a shower and get ready for another sunset at the canyon. We didn't plan this but that morning I forgot to mention I bumped into the Canadian's and had a convo about both our days and decided to meet up at the canyon together to watch it again.

Oh Mr. book, I wish you could mind read to give my fucking fingers a rest, but long story short, I met the Canadian's on my own, just after the sunrise experience and really did not want to invite them to watch our sunset number two, because Bolly has already told me she fancies the pants off one of them, and with her adventurous past, I was obviously not happy about any of this, nevertheless they were good guys, and paranoid Pete in me did not want to come out, so we met the Canadians and really enjoyed the sunset together. That night we went to the hostel 'Giants' we was meant to go to the night before. It was a wicked night, met some really cool people and got a little drunk, which I haven't done in a while, but like a book could read Bolly that night and the next day, because she was so distant, and in her head, really was hoping she didn't get her Indian visa, because not only was she all of a sudden a new born vegetarian, but a new born lesbian. I know I shouldn't judge or make accusations but she just isn't the same. Anyhoo, after a long silent day, we had a smoke with the Canadians on our last night, but unfortunately was so fucking ill, which probably had something to do with the freezing cold sunrise and getting burnt the same day. We went to bed early and caught a ride back to Bangkok the following day.

Personally one of the worst journeys of my life. It was a four hour mini cab ride up and down the mountains to Chaingmai in the pissing down rain, the tyres on the bus were so bald, it was sliding all over the place, then once we made it to Changmai, we had to hurry up in a Tuk Tuk, to get to the bus station to get our twelve hour bus ride to Bangkok. Luckily we made it to the bus on time, but got completely drenched in the process, so lovely twelve hour bus ride was in store for us, dripping wet. On board this bus a few hours into the journey a load of policeman got on the bus asking for peoples I.D, Bolly was asleep for this and I just glanced out of the window acting dumb, because my passport was obviously in Bangkok and didn't have any other I.D. Luckily the old bill didn't batter an eyelid at me, it seemed they were only interested in local Thai dudes, but once we got moving again I could hear them downstairs rustling through peoples bags and I've heard stories about westerners getting set up by old bill, planting drugs in peoples bags. So now I'm on edge, proper shitting my pants as half hour later the bus pulls over and a load of army dudes jumped on with a load of policemen, all strapped with machine guns. This time round I pretended to be asleep, in the end I was worrying over nothing, because they just done another round of I.D checks, and fucked off. Bolly bless her slept through the whole thing.

We arrived in Bangkok about 7am. Took a long walk round, Khoasan road looking for a place to stay, but was fucking mission impossible, as everything was fully booked. Luckily we found a place, it was a shithole and well above our budget, but could not be bothered to keep looking, so took it. Once we had a little sleep, shit, shave and shower, we got a taxi to the Indian embassy to get our passports back. It was a very tense and nerve racking hour, knowing our journey could have come to an end. Luckily we both received our visas, thank fuck. All this worry for nothing, we celebrated with a domino's pizza. So all is good, and we finally know we are both going India. We got back to Khoasan road and booked our flights to Chennai for the following day. Our last night and day in Bangkok mainly involved shopping and laundry, and a bit of research into India, as we know fuck all about the place. So we said goodbye to Thailand, and boarded our three hour flight to Chennai.

Well fuck me hello India. I had two questions as soon as we walked out the airport, what the fuck is everyone beeping their cars for? And what the fuck is that smell? This place is just mad, I thought Bangkok's traffic was crazy, this was just insane. The roads have no markings, no lanes, it is literally free for all. Still agree just like I said in Bangkok, it works better this way, the traffic flows a lot better than it flows in London. On the Friday night we arrived, we checked into our room 'Malaka residency', love the name. Apart from the stained sheets and the hole in the floor for a toilet, it weren't so sad. We were both starving and dying for a cigarette, but fuck all was open at midnight, so we tried our hardest to cut out all the noise coming from Indians music, screaming down the corridors, and the continuous bleeping from the cars outside, and tried getting some sleep. We managed to get a few hours, but I'm guessing a few hours is good for this place.

We took a walk round looking for somewhere to eat, or just buy fags, but could not see or spot anything, it was weird, we was in the middle of the over populated, loud, concrete jungle and couldn't find any shops. Funny really, there's so many Indian corner shops in London, but couldn't find one here. Luckily we came across some dude with a shop selling mobile phones, who also sold fags and water, which was a touch. Still desperately in need of toilet roll, but that will just have to wait. Fed up with walking around lost, we jumped in a Tuk Tuk to the beach, hopefully in search for food. But all that was to offer was a market on the beach selling, things made from seashells, and a few thousand Indians swimming fully clothed in the sea. We went and sat down by the sea and were the only two white people in sight, it was so funny, everyone kept coming over to take pictures, I felt famous! After a few hours people watching we decided to get a Tuk Tuk to central station, hoping we will come across some food. Luckily there were a chain of hotels down the station road, which had a few restaurants beneath them. Not knowing what to order, we just kinda pointed at a few things on the menu hoping for the best. Luckily the waiter see we had just arrived because he bought over a couple of spoons, once he see us staring at our food not wanting to munch with our hands, weird experience, but lovely food.

We got back to our digs and started to research on how to get the fuck out of Chennai, as it was far too crazy for our first day. Luckily our room had Wi-Fi, so we were able to find out what bus goes south and where to get it from. We looked up a place just a few hours south of Chennai called Mallupapurum'. Our plan was to catch the two local buses that goes there, but when we checked out the next morning and tried to explain to the tuk tuk driver, where the first bus was leaving from, we was in a pickle, because he didn't have a clue, and neither did the ten other blokes that was now surrounding us and the tuk tuk. So after much debate, of some really broken down English, we decided to get the tuk tuk to the second bus stop, because it wasn't far and he knew where it was. Our first local bus was such a good experience, we sat at the back with our backpacks and watch the bus fill up fast. It's so funny how many people they cram into these buses, and the bus doesn't actually stop at any bus stops, it just slows down so people can jump on and off of it. Thank fuck our stop was the last one, as I was not up for that. After a few pleasant hours talking to some locals on the bus, we arrived in Mallapapuram. After not much of a search, as we really could not be fucked to keep walking around in the heat, we checked into our sweat box. Again we had a hole in the floor for a toilet, and these sheets were better as they only had a few stains on them.

I fell in love with this place straight away as soon as I see restaurants and shops with toilet roll. Now I'm not a snob or even close, I mean I'm all game for shitting down holes, but a bit of loo roll goes along way. So once we had a shower with what only I can describe as a fitted garden hose with a broken head, ventured out to get some munch. We found a little restaurant, sat down and pretty much got told what we was having. They gave us a big leaf for a plate and slapped on some rice, bread and curry, with a couple of spoons bless em. Lovely food, I can't wait to learn to eat with my hands. After lunch we went trekking round the town and its temples to get our bearings. It's such a cool town, there are shit loads of cows, goats and dogs running around, along with bleeping buses, cars, tuk tuk's, rickshaws and horse and cart. We realised what all the beeping was about, no-one has or uses mirrors, so you have to beep to see or be seen. It was nice to see a few white faces around, as we were the only westerners in Chennai. We had a beer in some café, which was run by a guy, who just come and went as he pleased. I'm sure me and Bolly sat in this place unattended for over an hour, candle lit, as power cuts happen every five minutes here. Then we went and had another pukka munch with cutlery, but still struggling to order the right stuff, as we keep getting a truck load of dishes.

The next day we decided to go for a swim at the beach but once we got there we changed our minds, it stunk so bad. We just sat on the beach, avoiding the litter and lumps of shit, and had a nice few hours chatting to the locals as they passed. The Indian people are so nice, very very hospitable, always felt welcome, no matter where we were. It was at this beach we noticed a man washing his balls in the sea, but later we learnt he was probably having a shit and washing his ass. After the beach we managed to find a hotel with a swimming pool and chilled there for the day. Don't get me wrong, it's no beach, but had no old men having a dump, in front of you.

That evening we took a walk to our favourite coffee shop, where we met a few westerners we met the day before. They give us a few good tips on where to go and what to eat, we needed this advice as we were clueless. After coffee we looked for a place to eat and bumped into another group of westerners, who invited us to join them. They were a pukka group of people, four English dudes and one German chick, who all met in Chennai the day before. Some of them have been in India a while and give us some great tips on food, again well needed. After dinner we went back to their hostel for a little drink and smoke. The walk home for me and Bolly was proper fucked, at night India seems to shut down to let the wild dogs rule the streets. There were big packs of them running around tormenting cows and people. We managed to get home safe, after a slow walk with help from some locals. We could have easily of stayed here longer but only have eight weeks to see as much as India as possible, so unfortunately have to keep going. We got another local bus further south to a French colonized town called Pondicherry. This bus was more of a ball ache, because we wasn't first on like last time, so had to squeeze down the aisle with our backpacks and stand for a bit until a seat became available. It's fucking hard work being squeezed into a bus with a backpack, hand luggage and a guitar, whilst everyone perves at your missus. Luckily enough got ourselves a seat most of the way, thank fuck.

We arrived in Pondicherry with no research done on the place, so didn't have a clue where we were going. All we knew that there was a French settlement by the sea that we wanted to check out before boarding our bus to Madurai the following day. So we got a Tuk Tuk to take us there from the bus station, and had a long hard stroll round in the blistering heat trying to find a room, but everything was fully booked, story of my life, going to a place fully booked with no-one around. We finally found a guest house outside Frenchville, definitely the grottiest, weirdest place yet. Indian hotels and guest houses are the perfect setting for a scary movie. We had a shit, shave and shower and went to see all the boring French shit we needed to see. I had a few beers in 'la space', while Bolly skype'd her mum. We then went and had a walk around the city to have a look what to eat. On the way we bumped into some yank from California, and he was on the hunt for munch as well, so all three of us found some grotty looking shack selling Thali. It was the first time me and Bolly ate with our hands and we loved it. Definitely gonna take some practice not to get messy, but the food was good. All three of us got stuffed for 80p each. Walking home was a nightmare, I can't explain how fucked the traffic is. It's a non-stop flow, it's fucking free for all for pedestrians as well. You can't hesitate, if you see a gap you take it. We managed to get home in one piece and had a half decent sleep in the hotel from hell.

When we woke to discover we were still alive, and not been robbed, we went and done some exploring in Frenchville. We walked so far we ended up in the back roads of some Indian slums. The slums are always intimidating, but Indians are so friendly, I always feel safe. We had to get back to the hotel to get our bags, then jumped on a Tuk Tuk to take us to the bus station. When we booked this bus in the last town, Mallapapuram, we had no idea where we were going, and there were three places in Pondicherry to meet the bus. So we picked the bus stop Aravind hospital, thinking a hospital would be easy to find. To be honest it was easy to find, it just took ages to get there and once we realized it wasn't a bus stop, just a muddy patch on the side of a busy road, we regretted picking the hospital. Some Indian guy see us sitting there in complete confusion about whether or not this bus would turn up, and offered to phone the bus company for us, to reassure it was coming. Whilst this was going on, we had to change spots on the lovely motorway floor, because some dude with a couple of buffalo's with a trailer of sand decided he wanted to dump the sand where we were sitting. Its pitch black at this point. So not only, is it hard to see a bus come with fuck all street lights, we now have some random, his two friends, and a sand pit blocking our view. Luckily the guy who phoned the company for us, stopped the bus as it arrived two hours later. We could not have thanked him enough, love how welcomed and looked after we are here. Our bus was a bunk bed bus, fucking best bus I've ever been on, we had a double bed, top bunk, with a curtain, nightlight and plug socket, happy days. We both managed to get some sleep, fuck knows how, because every time we went over a bump, I smashed my head on the roof, still, only six hours later and we arrived in Madurai, at something stupid like four in the morning.

Again we arrived in a place, not having a clue where to go. Some Tuk Tuk bloke popped out from nowhere offering to take us to a cheap guest house, usually we don't like getting in Tuk Tuk's straight away, as normally there are after something, but it was pitch black and we have had a weird 24 hours, so we went with this dude to our new digs. No-one could really speak a word of English, when we arrived at this guest house, and it took over half an hour to check in. I've got over the fact about toilets and sheets, just gonna have to get used to the fact that you really do get what you pay for, because we aint really had a room for over three quid each yet. We had a shower and a little snooze, just before India wakes up and starts polluting noise massively.

We woke up and as you do on your first day, walked forever getting your bearings. It's weird I haven't actually lost Bolly yet. The streets are mad, so much to see and watch, biggest culture shock ever, India has turned out to be. We found a random shop that sold Cadburys chocolate, pop tarts, Werthers originals, all sorts of shit. As much as I've enjoyed the Indian food and tonnes of water, really thought I should treat myself here. It's funny, spending three quid on a room and a tenna on chocolate, I've never got the hang of priorities. We got our goodies and jumped in a Tuk Tuk to see Gandhi memorial. I thought I was gonna be bored shitless, but it was a very interesting museum of the history of India, and how the English, pretty much came and fucked it, like a lot of the world, when the empire was going strong. Got to love the English, never a dull story about a place that we visited in the past. We spent quite a while learning about good old Gandhi, then got a Tuk Tuk back to town. On the way we stopped for some cigarettes, I asked for a twenty pack, and every twenty pack he opened had loads missing from it, it was hilarious watching them all argue and rush trying to take cigarettes out of other boxes and trying to fill mine up. When we got back we found an amazing restaurant that served a pukka meal. It's like a Thali, where you get loads of different curry's and sauces, with chapatti's and poppadum's all for a pound.

There's a festival going on in Madurai at the moment so it's busier than normal. So me and Bolly have been searching for somewhere better and cheaper to stay, but we have had no hope. Whilst we was searching, we come to the Sri Meenakshi temple. The whole city is built around this temple, it's huge. About six hectares in total with grounds, and was twelve massive towers built from stone, covered in markings and painted in all different bright florescent colours. The marking involved gods, goddesses, demons and heroes, which scared the fucking shit out of me, I don't know about anyone else. The temple was buzzing this night as it was the night of the festival, and lucky enough, we got to stand on the roof of some weird sculpture shop, to see all the temple grounds lit up. You could hear Indian music blaring, the sound of the roads that surrounded us, abit of a Sagapo my life moment. We had to hurry up and get out of this place because the sculpture shop probably thought me and Bolly were a couple of rich westerners and were planning to buy something once we had finished on the roof, but little did they know we were skint backpackers, looking for a nice view of the city.

The next day we woke up and decided to go temple trekking. The first temple we got to had a huge elephant inside it, it was awesome, people were coming in having a prayer and being blessed by nelly the elephant. Such a cool experience to watch. Once nelly left, we left with him as it just wasn't the same without him. So we then went walking a little further and came across Sri Meenakashi, the big one we see last night. To be honest I couldn't wait to get in, to get away from the sun. We are fully clothed because you can't show skin in India, especially in temples, and was sweating my bollox off. After sticking our shoes in another temple shoe box, similar to what you get at the bowling alley, we got in. Bolly had to get re-dressed by some Hindu woman to look more covered up than she already was. Wow! What a temple, the best one I've seen so far. It was huge, we could have easily have spent all day there. The marking and painting inside were out of this world, I felt like I was in Indiana jones temple of doom. We had a long walk around its grounds and come across loads of cows, but these were not ordinary cows, they give you good karma if you fed them. So fuck it, we walked bare foot around the cows feeding them. Nothing better knowing once we have put our hands near the mouth of disease whilst knee deep in cow shit, we get good karma. We left that temple in search for a munch and decided to go back to the same restaurant we went to the day before. It was a wise choice, because this food was so good and we are getting better at eating with our hands. We got to bed quite early again, mainly because there's fuck all to do of a night.

The next day was just a day of fucking about deciding on where to go next and how to get there. We decided to take someone's advice, we met in mallapuram, and go south to Rameswaram. Our plan is to eventually get to the west coast and start heading north, but fuck it we thought we would treat ourselves to a few days further south. Rameswaram is only 20k away from Sri Lanka, so we know it's going to be hot. We got to the train station a good hour before it left, to get a good seat, and good job we did, because it got packed quickly. We shared an 8 seater booth with an Indian family who were very hospitable with the worst English going. It took 3 and a half hours to get there, and what a random journey it was. Every stop, Indians were getting on selling all kinds of food and chai tea. It was great, the Indian family insisted to buy us stuff and sort us out clean water.

As we pulled into Rameswaram, it was a bridge, as it's an island, and at the doors either side was a drop into the ocean, scary but beautiful. Once we left the train station, it didn't take us long to find a room. I was actually quite impressed with the room, it had a toilet seat, a long mirror and a garden with a washing line. So we can finally do some washing, as everything we have stinks, it was a tiny island, with a few small villages on it, but as me and Bolly roll, didn't know how big the island was, or even where about's we were on it. So we had a wonder for an internet café to google where the fuck we was, but this place was the most unwesternised place yet. It was covered in shit (litter) and hundreds of cows and goats running around, but to me, this is what I'm searching for. Someplace with now tourists, no-one speaking English, real authentistic India. We did manage to find one computer in some random shop, but forgot to google map and just told family back home we were safe. We decided to look for a laundry place and by chance we found a little shack doing laundry, but because there was a festival on in Rameswarum, he was too busy. Just our luck, turn up to a place with a festival, such a cool experience though, I can't explain to you how many people were in this tiny town. This town again was built around a temple, so walking round it was very hard work. Bolly actually got hit by a bus, it was jokes, obviously she didn't find it funny, but me and a few other Indian dudes did.

I see some weird shit on this day. A motorbike with a cage hanging off the back with a good 30 live chickens inside, three women standing on the side of the road having a piss together, and just a lot of unexplainable weird shit. The boyfriend/girlfriend relationship is hard to understand for Indians, as many times we have been asked are we married, and when we reply together we are not married they just don't understand, and because of this Bolly has been proposed to so many times it's a joke. It's hilarious when she replies no, because they proper get the ump about it. We had a really cool first day exploring through thousands of religious festival goers, watching them cleanse their sins in water I would not even like to dip my toe in. We decided to hand wash our clothes, so we bought a bucket and some powder and hung it out in our garden, happy fucking days.

We woke up the in the morning craving for a beach, and because of all the rules about covering yourself up and all the perverts floating about we decided to find the most secluded beach possible. So we got in a Tuk Tuk and drove 20k to a tiny village. This village was the most beautiful but poorest village I've ever seen. All the little houses were smaller than six foot and were made out of old bits of bamboo and leaves. We were once again the only westerners in sight, so we had a good long walk to a spot where Bolly was comfortable to sunbath in her bikini. We chilled out for a few hours, as much as we enjoyed the beach and being able to swim, the wind was too strong and the sand really fucking hurt, spraying up our backs. Plus a big group of Indian guys decided to sit 10 meters away blatantly for a perve, so we decided to get up and head back. We told our Tuk Tuk just to drop us off, as we didn't want to pay for him to wait, but that turned out to be a wrong decision. As everyone else here had rides back but us, and the local pick-up truck bus was nowhere to be seen, so as we was sitting there like two lost puppies some random guy said he's heading back with his missus and mother-in-law and there was a few spaces for us, happy days.

While we were waiting we spoke to some French dude who told us you can get on a 4x4 and go even further to a more secluded town. So we decided to come back the next day and take his advice to explore. When we got back and had a shower, we had a walk round the city temple again to see it without all the crowds on festival day. The temple was beautiful, it reminded me of a smaller version of the one we see in Madurai. Whilst in this temple we met an Indian man selling weed. We have constantly been getting asked if we wanted weed since we have been in India, but always been worried about old bill, but I got a good vibe from the dude and treated myself to a big bag. It was intimidating and very sketchy drug deal, but went perfectly ok, thank fuck! So straight away, we went back to the room for a few sneaky ones. Unfortunately we had no rolling papers, and no-one in this town sells them, so we had to empty a cigarette out to re fill it with weed, which was a complete ball ache, but well worth the hassle.

The following morning we went for breakfast and to find out where to get the bus from to get back to the beach, as a Tuk Tuk is overpriced. While we were walking around, we bumped into a few guys we had dinner with in Mallupaprum, so we gave them our guest house name and told them we were off to the beach, so they checked in and decided to join us. It's really nice to have company, as me and Bolly have been in each other's pockets, and being that there was 5 of us, we all split a Tuk Tuk, so we didn't have to get a bus. Once we got to the town, we wanted to get the 4x4 to the next village, but there wasn't many people about today, and it's a lot cheaper if they fill it up, so we waited for more people to turn up and success it was. It was us 5 and probably 15 other Indians cramped onto the back of this 4x4 pick-up truck. What a mad journey it was, we drove over sands dunes and spent a lot of the journey in the sea, hell of a bumpy ride. When we got to the village it was like looking at a polish town after ww2, all the tiny buildings and churches were completely flattened, all were in ruins. It was because of a cyclone 20 years ago, and now all is left for the fisherman to survive in, are these huts made from drift wood and leaves.

We all sat by the sea and had a little dip, for a few hours, then from afar we could see a storm rolling in. Within the matter of minutes the sky went from blue to black and started pissing down. The rain was so fast and heavy, we literally couldn't see 10 feet in front of us. The only shelter that was on offer was a few random bamboo huts, which was leaking so bad and already had 30-40 Indians standing under it. As the rain died down the Indians told us to make a run for the 4x4 as it's only going to get worse. So we run back to where we left our pick-up truck, and it was no-where to be seen. It didn't look like we could get back, which no-one was worried about because it would have been quite cool to stay with some of the locals in there huts. Then after about half hour wait in the pouring down rain, the 4x4 pulled up and told us to jump in, happy days.

The funny thing was, this guy didn't just drive back to where we needed to go, he took us further into the village for a little pit stop for himself, and parked the truck out in the open. The rain was coming in sideways at this point, we were drenched. After the bloke stood under a shelter and watched us get soaked, he invited us into his mum's house to dry off. It was a lovely offer, just 20 mins too late. We waited in this hut for almost half an hour, then the driver told us he was ready to go, and once we got back to the 4x4, it was ram packed with massive fish and giant squid. This journey home was the most, wettest, smelliest, most uncomfortable journey of my travels, but definitely one for the journal. We got back to our guest house after an hour of rain and fish, and all desperately needed a shower.

When we got back to Rameswaram, it was flooded. Literally knee deep roads, couldn't give a fuck to be honest, I was already soaking wet, the only problem was, when it floods in Asia (especially India) all the sewage pops up to play. So not only did we stink of fish, we now smelt of maggots and shit. Oh the joys of travelling. Once we had a shower, we all went for dinner, it was good being with the guys, as they have been here for a few months and give us some advice on what the words meant on the menu, which is a touch because we have been ordering food not knowing what's going to come out, it's fun to do but I've lost so much weight. After dinner we found a bar, this bar was the seediest, dingiest place I've ever drunk in, but was well worth the experience. Bolly was getting looks left, right and center, as she was the only woman in sight. To be honest, India can be described in one word (Men). There are hardly any women, anywhere, I've come to a conclusion, that you never see a pregnant woman in India, and for the population I'm guessing, woman are pregnant a lot, so pregnant woman must just stay in. No-one really smokes in India, don't get me wrong, they love a joint, but no fags. I think it's forbidden for woman to smoke, because every time Bolly lights up a smoke, she gets the most evil looks from people, especially woman. We woke up the next day and done abit of research on where to go next and when. All 5 of us decided to get the train back to Madurai the following morning to catch a bus from there that evening to the west coast, to a place called Kochi.

Our last day in Rameswaram was a slow day of getting rid of the smell of fish and watching movies, as the weather is still shit. We only had a few hours' sleep as we had to be up for 4.30am. It was this train journey that got to me the most, emotionally for mine and Bolly's melting relationship. We sat separately, by her choice, wanting to sit opposite one of the guys we was with, and the whole journey I could see them, gazing into each other's eyes, having a laugh. Which hasn't been the case for me and Bolly for a while, and no longer has the love for me she did. It breaks my heart to see her flirt with other guys, especially when things are not great between us.

Journal 4

Hello book number 4, how the fuck are you. I would like to say thank you Lara 'Bollys mum', for getting me this journal for my birthday. So we are now back in Madurai, but only for the day as we are leaving for Kochi in the evening. As we got out the train station, me and Ben had a scout on times and prices for buses to Kochi, while Bill and Mitch had a scout for times and prices for trains, and Bolly sat and waited with the bags. When we got back to Bolly and the bags, we came to the decision to get a bus, as it was cheaper and arrived in Kochi at a sensible time. We were able to leave our bags with the booking office, which was a touch because we had all day to hang about. I had a plan to book a few days in Kochi on a houseboat around the backwaters, which are a shit load of canals and rivers, which run through a load of villages. Plus it was Valentine's Day tomorrow and thought it could be a good few days for me and Bolly to get some romance back in our lives. But Bolly would you believe it, decided to invite the guys along, just as she invited them to travel to the west with us. It's been killing me that she no-longer enjoys my company, I think we really should have gone our separate ways in Thailand, to save what we have left on this downhill relationship.

We ended up having a really cool day, walking around the town, temple trekking, we even treated ourselves to a few brandy's in a bar we found. This bar was actually very modern, not like the one in Rameswaram, which was more like a sess pit, in an old ancient burial tomb. We had to walk to our bus in the pissing down rain, it wasn't very far, but we got drenched. I was honestly thinking about saying to Bolly, that we should travel separately for abit, as we were growing further and further apart, but knowing its valentine's day tomorrow, and the fact that I didn't want to leave her with some dude I was jealous of her flirting with. So on the bus I got, and slept the whole 8 hour journey, thanks to a little help of valium. Best night's sleep I've had in a long while.

We arrived in Kochi about 9am and got a Tuk Tuk to fort Kochi, which is the place to be, supposingly, thanks to the great travel guide lovely planet. We all sat and had coffee while Bill had a scout about for a cheap room. We managed to find a few rooms, next to each other with a communal balcony, that the landlord didn't mind us smoking weed on, probably because he was always constantly high. I had a shower and got ready before anyone else, so I decided to go and have a walk round to get my bearings, and get Bolly a present for valentines. I love this town, Kochi is an Old Portuguese settlement, with some amazing buildings and churches. It's the cleanest place I've been to yet in India, there's no litter, not as many homeless, and no-one taking a dump on the side of the road, but is over-run by westerners on holiday, which I don't mind seeing, but just really doesn't feel like India.

Well as far as Valentine's Day go, this one was most definitely my worst one ever. Me and Bolly are completely opposite when it comes to romance, I'm a complete soppy bastard, where Bolly is as tough as nails and cringes at anything romantic. So once I got back to the gaff, me and Bolly went for a walk, sit and a talk down by the riverside. I could have cut the tension with a knife, she just doesn't smile at me like she used to, never kisses me and actually sometimes pulls away when I go to kiss her. So after an hour of absolute agony, we went back to the gaff, and got ready for dinner. Our Valentine's Day dinner, was just as awkward as the day, shit.

I'm not an idiot, I can read Bolly like a book, and I know deep down, not only does she no longer have love for me, she now had another dude in mind. We got back to the gaff and met up with the guys and had a good smoke. Personally I would have rather have spent my valentines night having sex for as long as possible, but no not Bolly, she would rather get high and flirt some more in front of my face with Ben. That night we had the most awkward spoon and sleep. I could not sleep, all I wanted to do is go into the next room, cut off Ben's head, blend it into a masala, and make bolly eat it.

The next morning, I had had enough, as soon as we woke, I said we need to talk, so we went on the rooftop and spoke some home truths, I asked her time and time again, did she want to be with me and she always replied yes, so we came to an agreement to travel alone for a few weeks, hoping it would do us good. I made it clear to her as well, on how much her constant flirting with Ben was doing my head in, so told her to back off, but Bolly as I could of guessed was in denial and didn't realise she was. So we decided she was going Gokana and I was going to Goa and that day we all went to the train station together to book trains out of Kochi. Bolly managed to get a train to Gokarna the following night, and would you believe it, Bill and Ben were going Gokana the night after, I managed to get a train booked to Goa the next day, which takes 15 and a half hours. Yay I can't wait to sit on a train, for over 15 hours thinking about how my missus is probably getting spit roasted by fucking Bill and Ben the flowerpot men. Our last day together we all decided to take a walk round a load of art galleries, which was really cool, but I had too much on my mind and could not stand to be around Bolly and Ben, so I left the 3some to it, went back to the room, where Mitch was sitting with a sprained ankle and dragged him to a pub with me. After a beer, I felt instantly better, and started thinking about me and my trip more than Bolly. Saying buy to Bolly that night, was one of the hardest things I've ever done. I know absence makes the heart grow fonder, but because of how much I'm in love with divvy bollox, I didn't need my heart fonder. I just hope and pray this time apart will give bolly a slap in the face on how good I am to her. It really breaks my heart leaving her on her own, knowing how many perverts are out there. I know you're gonna think I'm a sad cunt book number 4, but fuck you if ya do, because on the Sunday morning day of my train, I actually went into a church and prayed for Bollys safety, so that's, that, there's nothing more I can do, and Mr bible of wisdom, just to let you know, I'm finally up to date with you.

I'm now sitting on my 15 and half hour train journey to Goa. I've got myself a sleeper, which is a bunk bed, so hopefully with the help from my friend valium, I will be able to get some sleep, but I need to set an alarm for roughly 3am, because that's the time it gets to Goa, and if I sleep through, there's a chance I could end up in the Himalayas. So wish me luck ya big fat get.

Hello again! I'm still on this fucking train, it's only been 5 hours and I'm bored out my nut, I was keeping myself busy sitting down, hanging out of the doors, but the suns fucked off now, and I can't see nothing. However I was gobsmacked at some of the Indian countryside. It's amazing, millions of palm trees scattered across all the farmland with farmers playing football and cricket. I've passed rice paddies and spice and tea plantations that makes the landscape look so good it looks fake. I've also passed quite a few small and poor slums covered in litter. No matter where in India you go, whether it be a city, a small town or a beach, it's covered in litter and shit. Just a minute ago, the ticket inspector got on and told me I was in the wrong carriage, so I had to walk down several carriages. I think I got stared at by every single person on this train, the carriages are so long it felt like I was never going to find my correct sleeper bunk, but success it was, when 1 man see me stressed and confused. He looked at my ticket and pointed my in the right direction, I'm a but gutted, because I started to get to know the Indian family sitting next to me at my old seat, oh well, I will just have to make new friends. I think I pretty much walked the whole length of this train and I'm definitely the only westerner on it, and just for the record, these sleeper bunks have got to be the most uncomfortable thing I've ever sat on let alone sleep on. I got in touch with a friend I know from kavos (Frenchy), and he lives and works in Goa and invited me to stay at his house, so I'm so looking forward to a proper bed and pillow, the more I sit and let me thoughts wander, the more I miss Bolly. I really can't wait to start my meditation and yoga, because I really need to clear my mind and stop pining over her.

Booky boy, well fuck me, all that talk about setting my alarm for 3am was a waste of time, because my phone got stolen on the train, I had left it beside my head like a complete Muppet and my bunk bed was head high, so anyone walking passed would have seen it. Luckily some old bird woke me up and asked where I was going, so I told her Margoa (train station in Goa), and she said this was the stop. I was freaking out because as she told me this the train started to pull off, so I chucked my bag and guitar out of the door and made a jump for it. It wasn't going fast, but fast enough for me to have to walk back down the platform 20 meters for my stuff. I was in a pickle, I wasn't sure if I had left anything behind, didn't have a clue what the time was, or even if this was truly my stop. Once all the Indians on the platform stop laughing at me, and I regrouped my things and walked out the station to discover it was the right place and it was 4am, my heart beat instantly slowed down and I started cracking up to myself. I walked to the taxi stand to get a ride to Paloloem beach, which is where my new humble abode was waiting, and I was gobsmacked at the price! Normally with the Tuk Tuk you can barter a price, but taxi's outside train stations are fixed expensive prices. Just to give you an idea on what I mean, the train I just got was 1050k and cost me 500 rupees, and the taxi I got to the beach, which was 40k away cost me 900 rupees, it's still only about 10 quid, but pounds I don't have and rupees I do have, so fuck you taxi man.

I managed to find Frenchys house ok, but what I didn't know is that he has a dog, a very loud dog, and as I opened the front gate I set it off. The fucking thing scared the shit out of me, and unfortunately woke everyone up. After a very tired and awkward intro to Frenchy and his house mate, I was shown my room and went straight to bed. I woke up to see my new house, it was a 5 bedroom house on the beach, I had 1 room, frenchy and his missus Vicky had another room, and met some guy vaguely last night in another room. So I'm still to meet the other 2 room-mates, if there are. It was a shared bathroom and kitchen which were both spotless, thank fuck I'm finally living with tidy people, as Bolly can be a very untidy and grubby bitch at times. I went for a wander after a shower to get my bearings and breakfast, and instantly feel in love with this place. Our house is smack bang in the middle of this beach, which is out of this world, white sands, blue seas, swimmable water, because of the bay it's in, so no rip tides, and all surrounded by palm trees, that backs onto a very hippy little town. I've landed right on my feet here, I know it's only my first day, but I might spend my last 6 weeks in India here. Fuck it I know when I was in Thailand, I hated westerners and drunken fools, and appreciated northern Thailand and east India, because it's off the beaten track, with no white people in sight, but deep down I love meeting travellers and making new friends, and this seems the place for that.

When I got back to the house to get ready for the beach, I met Vicky and 2 of her friends, a guy and a girl who work in Palolem beach as well. The chick was telling me about the parties here, and it sounds like a right bit of me. No more worrying about getting drunk and upsetting the missus, I'm gonna get out my nut, for the next 6 weeks, fuck it. Do you know what book' Sagapo my life a little bit'. ++++++++++Missing part of the Journal, sorry can literally, make no sense, of my own hand writing, in a nutshell it's a drunken love my life moment +++++++++++++++++++++++++

Oh bloody hell, why didn't I just fly straight here from Bangkok, it is so fucking sweet, the guys I live with are absolute nutters. Frenchy and a group of adrenaline junkies are tour guides for Canyoning. This is an activity that involves, Rock Climbing, Absailing and Cliff Jumping. They go through national parks, up and down waterfalls and caves. I'm going to book myself a few courses on the extreme package. These jumps are over 20 meters, and some of the absailing is 100 meters, I pushed myself to a limit when I climbed Mt Rinjani on Lombok, and believe my limits could exceed that. This canyoning malarkey is a right bit of me. Its nuts. Today the guys had the day off, but still decided to get up early and go for a trek. We swam over to monkey island, and rock climbed around the whole thing, no safety harness, nothing, proper bear grilles style, it was the nuts. Some of the drops, were no doubt complete death if were to happen, but were the best bits. We had to cliff jump and swim into a cave, to get up and over the other side. Was only a 6 meter jump, but such a buzz and a nice little taster of what's to come. The cave here can be absailed into from the top of the island, but we had no torches or equipment, I literally had my converse and a pair of shorts on. Obviously when they are canyoning, they have ropes, harnesses, torches and shit, but I like it like this.

I got back from my morning trek and had a good smoke with a few randomers at the house, I love living here, its where all the workers seem to come and hang out. The girl I met the other day is a flyerer, she gives out flyers for a number of things, and one of them is yoga. So I took a little walk to this yoga retreat, to check it out. The walk there was amazing, it was through small hippy shanty towns, round tiny beaches with only one shop on each. I really can't describe the beauty of it. It took me about half an hour to get there, and the woman there was very inviting, helpful and friendly. The majority of people I've met, are over 30 and English. It seems to me, this is the place people come to settle down, once travelled enough. I keep seeing me in some of these old boys, and it puts a big smile on my face, as these guys are very happy and content with life, which is all I want. I'm looking forward to starting yoga, just to do that walk every day. I have got a scooter, and there is a road/dirt track, to get there in case I get lazy.

Last night was a good laugh, there was about 8 of us, and we all drove to some random restaurant in the pitch black. We had an amazing meal and smoked something called a chillum, it's basically a bong made out of a certain plant. This palm tree looking bong messed me up and made the drive home a lot more interesting. I love this life style, there's no laws or policing, just everyone getting on in peace and happiness. It's a shame, Bolly would have loved it here, I really miss her, I hope she is safe and happy, I'm sure she is, as she is in gokarna, which is only a few beaches down and I'm guessing its similar there.

Fuck kinnnelllllll, canyoning is fucking awesome. I went on a half day trip yesterday, and going on a full day one tomorrow. I'm so jealous of the jobs these guys have got. Absailing down waterfalls for me, pisses all over skydiving. I done something called the spider drop, it's when you absail over a waterfalls cliff edge, and there's fuck all beneath or around you, just one hell of a drop into the washing machine below. You then absail down a rope as far as it goes, then just let go and drop. Dangling there getting smashed by the falling water is fucking hard work. I can't believe how much shit we done on a half day, I'm proper buzzing for this full day. The amount of jumps we did was a joke. The biggest was only 10 meters, but some of them you had to run and jump off of to reach the tiny pool below. There were a couple of girls on this day, that didn't want to do some of the jumps, and some you don't have to jump, but some you do. Watching some French chick get told she has to jump or climb back up was hilarious, she was f'ing and blinding in French. It was sexy as fuck to be honest, listening to her freak out in French, but could not stop laughing. Everyone else on the tour was sweet as, two girls from England, and a couple (guy from England, and a girl from Germany), none of them had ever done something like this before, but all did really well. Really good day out, the canyons we went to were in a national park, with a lot of dangerous wildlife, including Tigers, but no luck, didn't see anything apart from big ass cows, that charge at you whether you're walking or in a car. The landscape is the fucking nuts, when you get quite high up there are some viewpoints that look down on the jungle and all its beaches along the west coast. No photo would do any justice for this view. India is a beautiful country, it's just a shame it got infected with humans. Not just ya average human, dirty smelly ones that love to spit, piss and shit everywhere.

As much as I love this canyoning, I don't think I could do it for a living, I'm not getting any younger, and the way I've abused my body in the last 10 years, I would be well and truly fucked after two weeks, but its definitely something I want to start looking into. I mean don't get me wrong, I love a good temple, and learning about countries and cultures, but climbing Mt. Rinjani and Goa'n canyoning is a right bit of me. Next trip I go on, I'm fucking off the tourist track completely and going to get myself lost in a jungle or island somewhere. I feel so alive right now, I always used to envy couples travelling, I remember when me and Matty used to talk about it. He used to say travelling with ya missus is the worst thing, and I always disagreed, and wanted it a lot, and now I've experienced it, I'm afraid to say it's absolutely horse shit. Matty was right all along, travelling with ya missus sucks balls. I have no worries, no bitching, and no decisions on things trying to please someone else. It's just a shame, I fell in love with someone whilst doing it. Fuck I really miss that divvy prat.

What's crackalackin, oh my god the full day smashed it. To start the day we all had a wake and bake, which made the journey there a lot more interesting. It takes an hour and a half up and down mountains, and round some of the tightest corners I've ever drove, and when a speeding bus comes flying round one of these bends, its fucking scary, especially when your high. We made it there ok thank fuck. Oh and I saw my first mongoose on the drive, it was a big bastard, good job I didn't hit it, I think I would have come off worse. Doing the first half of this day was so funny, when your high, every jump seems so much higher than they were a few days ago. What a fucking buzz, this canyoning is, most of the jumps in this canyon you touch the floor because the pools are not that deep, so they told me to be as loose as possible because I will touch the floor. It didn't bother me too much the first time I done it, but this time round, frenchy took me away from the other tourists, up cliffs to get to bigger jumps, and when you hit the floor from these heights, you fucking know about it. Frenchy and Mark the crazy fucks were doing summer sorts and backflips. Fuck that for a laugh, I struggle to jump in the right spots at the best of times, especially the jumps where you have to take a run up. No, just a good old fashioned one hand on my nose, the other on my nob works fine for me.

The second part of this day was awesome, we had lunch half way down this canyon, and from the boulder we sat on, we could see everything. Such a perfect spot to have lunch, and another bifta. I don't think the rest of the tourists with us were pleased that all the guides were getting high, but it's the end of the season, so no-one gives a shit anymore. There were no more jumps left, just two high absails to do. The first one I wasn't in control of, I think because of the height of it, and the size of the ropes we had. We have to be lowered by someone else, don't get me wrong, I trust the guides in what they do, but to not have control on my life and leaving it in control of a stonner was freaking me out abit, still an awesome absail. The second one, we was in control of, and this was a proper bit of me. I even had an audience at the bottom of the canyon, some large Indian family was sitting there getting drunk, probably hoping to see some westerners make a mistake. It was a proper sagapo my life moment, hanging half way down this waterfall, there was a spot where a boulder poked out which caused a gap in the waterfall, and this was well needed because I couldn't see a fucking thing. As I just hung there, I could see far out over the jungle, some of the trees moved because of the monkeys, I had Indian music being played by the piss heads below, just completely and utterly sagapo my life.

When all of us reached the bottom we drove to the local pub to celebrate. This place was a proper dive, it was like being back in that pub in Rameswaram, afraid to touch anything in case I ended up catching something. The group we had today was two German girls, some Aussie guy, some Scottish dude, and two polish lads. It was the polish who were not happy with us getting high all day, and we were now in a pub and these guys don't drink, bless em, they have not had the best day. Everyone jumped in the jeep and headed back to Palolem, me and Frenchy stayed for a few more before driving back. Frenchy was telling me that tomorrow, there was no one booked up, and that they had an exploration day planned. It was a day of discovering new canyons and routes to sell to tourists next year. This sounded sick. Untouched jungles, that only farmers have ever seen, and I'm guessing have never cliff jumped and absailed down, I was well up for it, especially when he told me we could get arrested, because it was a national park and we have no authorisation to be there. The boss said it was cheaper to get nicked than get permits, as he has been arrested many times in this jungle.

When we got back to Palolem, we met up with the Canyoning crew and a few other workers in the restaurant Vicky (frenchys missus) works in. Unfortunately frenchys boss turned up un invited. I see everyone's faces dropped as he entered, but didn't clock why, I've only met him a few times, and they have been very brief, but not long into the meal did I realise why everyone did not give him the biggest of welcomes. He is and absolute shit-cunt, I've never met a man so ignorant, so up himself, and so fucking rude. He looks like a fat French midget. Sorry he doesn't look like that, he actually is a fat French midget. So anyway we were all talking about the exploration day, and bearing in mind I'm pretty drunk by now, did not like what he had to say, so thought I would open my mouth, maybe abit too much. He was telling me, I can't smoke nowhere near him, if I can't keep a minimum of 80 kph on my bike, he would not wait and I would be lost. He even had the cheek to say, if it's my turn to jump first I have to jump, now I understand why the guys keep their mouths shut, because he does pay their wages, and I've been there when I've had to hold my tongue to an employer when he/she has been an absolute wank stain. But he is not my boss, I don't like ignorant people, especially ignorant French people, so I let him ave it. As you can imagine, wasn't best pleased, so there and then I decided I would not go with the guys exploring, well gutted because it sounds awesome, but personally would rather chill out on my lonesome all day on the beach, than spend the day with French Danny DeVito. Apart from French Danny, it was a real nice evening, I treated myself to a steak, as I haven't had beef since Australia, plus we were allowed to sit there and get high after dinner, which was sweet.

I woke up the next morning with really bad guts, probably because my body is not used to good food. I spent the day doing my own exploring up and down the coast, seeing some amazing beaches, I'm a big fan of the Goa'n coastline and all its friendly locals. If it wasn't riddled with disease and had a few more GETS floating about, I would happily live here. Talking of GETS, I can't get divvy bollox out of my head, I am trying to enjoy myself and forget about her, but all this time alone just makes me think a lot. The way she was with me the last month we were together, has finally dawned on me that we are over. It's a fucking weird feeling when you're travelling with someone you love, and have plans to move into a flat together when we got home, and go to sibling's weddings and shit. Then all of a sudden, your plans no longer mean shit and your world has been turned upside-down. Ahh its funny when you think about it, yesterday I was getting high jumping around Leopold infested Canyons, and today I'm sitting here in need of a cuddle from my mum, I'm a funny old fucker, and if this book ever is to become a movie, good luck to the guy playing my role.

Kinnnellllll book, I was on Skype to my bro Simon yesterday and the couple from the half day trek popped into the internet café and asked if I wanted to go for a few beers with them, so once we had all finished on the net we went to the beach for sunset. It was a lovely couple of hours, and we arranged to meet up that night with the other two English girls that were also on the half day trek, plus when I got back to the house the Canyoning crew was home and they were all down to go out and get on it. So a great night was planned, until I put my head on my pillow after a shower and woke up this morning. I see frenchy this morning before he went on another trip, he said he tried waking me up, but couldn't, what is wrong with me! Fuck I really am getting old!

I love waking up and going for breakfast here, the walk to my favourite café isn't very far, but I have to walk passed a few Indian women on the way, sitting outside their shops trying to sell me stuff. On my first day here I must have walked passed these old girls five or six times, and every time I got 'hello sir, look in my shop'. It was doing my nut in, so now every morning I get up and buy three chai teas from the shop opposite where I live and take them to my three favourites, so now all I get is a simple 'hello sir, have a nice day'. One of the old girls knows all about my travels and recently becoming single, so she told me to marry one of her daughters. She has eight girls and two boys, it was hilarious being introduced to all her girls, not one of them was over the age of 12, so I kindly refused and told her I might come back in ten year's time. One girl crack me up and said 'I will not wait ten years, I want many children, so need to start soon'. I was very high at the time, so this was kind of freaking me out, so cowardly this morning, I walked along the beach to my café, just in case the hungry pack of 10 year olds were out on a hunt, shame Scotty aint here, he would have loved it.

On the way back to the house I bumped into the Aussie dude who was on the full day tour with me. He was on his scooter and said he was going to take a ride to some northern beaches. I've only really explored the south and I was planning to just sit on the beach and get high all day, so I decided to tag along. It was an amazing drive, dangerous as fuck, but loads of fun. It's not just the millions of shit drivers here, it's the millions of cows wandering about, it's like Russian roulette whether you decide to speed past it or not. Fucking love these roads. I've always said traffic in Asia works because of the lack of laws, like lanes and traffic lights, and it's so true, I've never seen grid lock here for longer than a few minutes, it's completely free for all. When we got deep in the jungle we drove through an area called Leopold valley, and see signs warning people of Leopold's. I didn't see one. I hate the fact that all the coolest animals in the world are nocturnal. We got to see some beautiful untouched beaches, I do like a good beach, people say that when you've seen one beach you've seen em all. Well these people are talking shit, because this is the first time I've seen beaches with no people on it, just cows, goats and pigs running around. It was a weird drive, one minute you're in untouched paradise, the next you're in a village with massive piles of rubbish scattered about, people spitting and having a sneaky poo on the side of the road. The Aussie dude had this wicked little GPS, it picked up all the roads, as well as small dirt tracks, so we could go get ourselves lost without having to spend the night in the jungle. Yeah I've just named him Aussie dude because as introductions were made, like every time it went in one ear and straight out the other, so it's too late now to ask, fuck it.

We decided to head back after a good four hours exploring, there's no way in hell I'm driving back in the dark, especially the distance we have made by now. We got back in time to watch the sunset on the beach, it sets right over the top of Monkey Island, that's the island me and Frenchy climbed round the other day. And happy fucking days it's a full moon, so as that sun drops that moon rises. Last time I see this I was in Pai, in the freezing cold morning, sitting on top of a canyon. I love it, that morning I wanted the sun to hurry up and rise because I couldn't feel my fingers, and now I want it to fuck off, as I've been burnt to a crisp on that scooter all day.

Mr Journal of justice where have you been, I've neglected you for a while, as I'm slowly losing the plot. I've loved Goa, Palolem beach, and all the cool people I've met, but getting drunk on a beach with a load of workers has been done, I need a change of plan. I've not been too well physically and mentally, I've hit a brick wall with my digestive system, as I'm never hungry, but shit alot. To be honest that sounds like the story of my life, but Indian shits are like no other. Mentally I'm not in a good way, I can't get divvy bollox out of my head, first thing in the morning, last thing at night, in my dreams, lock stock, the fucking lot. So I've decided for some messed up strange reason I'm going to leave this tropical paradise and get into northern India's desert, 'Rajastan'. If I'm going to lose the plot I'm going to do it on the back of a camel, instead of on a beach full of happy people. I hope to god this doesn't happen, and have an awesome trip up to the north, but the way I'm feeling at the moment, as my brother Mat would say, 'fucking Coo Coo'. No seriously booky, I lost the plot years ago, the main reason I'm getting off my lazy ginger ass is all for you my journal of complete gibberish, there's no chance I'm letting the last month of the god all mighty journal of Oscar and Noah, become about a depressant man, on a two and half year bender. It's not happening, I'm going to pull my head out of my ass and explore. So my plan is to go to Hampi for a few days which is six hours inland from here, then head north to Mumbai for a few nights, before entering Rajastan.

Do you know what mate, I've been sitting here in some Greek bar/restaurant listening to some old 80's classics missing home more than I've ever done. My family are a big inspiration on my life and would not be here today without them, each one of my brothers has a slice of their personality in me in one way or another, my mum is basically me with tits, and my dad is basically me with bigger tits. As much as I'm missing them all, feel like they have been here with me. Don't get me wrong Skype end Facebook helps, but you know what I mean. Fucking miss em so much. Scotty I miss the most, there's no one in the world I've been through more than Scott, bless him the big gimp. I spoke to him the other day and he just sat through a cyclone, whilst in a roadhouse in Northwest Australia, still loving life. He has met up with Scouse Nicky, and is saving well, ready for the flight home for mat's wedding. He says he's been learning the guitar, but deep down know he aint taking a guitar to the wedding, as well as me. I've been driving around on my moped exploring what I've not yet seen on the west coast of Goa, and have been stopping off in coffee shops for a rest on the way, and it has just come to my attention that Indians are very gay, probably due to the fact there are no chicks anywhere. Talking of chicks, I'm going to a silent disco tonight, so I'm off on the pull, been doing my yoga, so am ready to stretch my body in ways it's never been stretched.

Well fuck me dead, I was talking about sex when I mentioned stretching, but the only stretching done on this night, was when I ended up in a bush on my way home, still sitting on the bike. I should never have drove there in the first place, it's only a 15 minute walk. We all said we would drive there and walk back, knowing full well that wasn't going to happen. Fucking awesome night though. Me and mark went for a few games of pool after a pre drink in the house with the northern lot. We met 3 dudes in this bar, Aussie, English and Irish. Who we invited back to the house for more drinking games. Once the rest got home from working late, we all ventured onto the silent disco. It went on till 4am, and with a little help from one of the northern girls tab of goodness, made it up till sunrise. This was the first time I've been completely 'Dogsh#!t' and having a dance, in a long time, really needed to get it out of my system. Fuck me did I pay for it the next day. I had a few injuries from my crash on the way home, hung-over, coming down, and to put the cherry on the cake, woke up without my favourite flip flops. I'm glad I got it out my system though, because I'm now on the wagon. I'm getting really concerned with my health, I'm never hungry and have been false feeding myself. Todays the day I leave Goa, and get a six hour bus to Hampi. If I don't get any better after Hampi, I'm going to fly home from

Mumbai. I'm in desperate need for a good solid western meal and a decent bed.

Fuck me, Hampi is the bollox. Its landscape is like something I've never seen before. It's a very old sacred city, that was thriving with life until about 500 hundred years ago, the Muslims invaded and smashed and burnt everything. There are ruins of temples and palaces everywhere, some that were discovered only 20 years ago. There are huge rocks and boulders spread all over the place, which have been sculptured into gods and goddesses by the Hindu's. Ugly fucking scary things if you ask me, but unbelievable craftsmanship has gone into them. The morning I got here, I got off the bus and took a walk to the river as I wanted to stay on the north side, as I've read it's the cheaper and nicer side. So once I had got to the boat to cross I was told by a group of people I was already on the north side, as the boat was pulling off. So these guys told me to stay at the guesthouse they were about to have breakfast in. So fuck it, I followed these guys and checked in to the most overpriced place on the wrong side of the river. I had breakfast with the guys and they invited me with them to go on a bike ride around the temples, happy days.

So me, a polish couple, a Dutch girl, a German girl, a Turkish guy and an American guy went on this mad bike ride. All of these people have met here in Hampi. We had to meet a tour guide who was renting us the bikes and giving us a brief history lesson on these heritage sites. The tour guide turned up with five more people, two Aussie dudes, two English chicks and an Irish bloke. It was such a good day, all 12 of us, riding up and down the hills of Hampi, surrounded by Banana, Mango and Coconut trees, covered with monkeys. I only put a bit of sunscreen on in the morning, so after a few hours I was quickly turning pink. The German and Dutch girl see this, and started pulling out scarves and bits of clothing to cover me up, bless em. After the trek, me, the Turk and the German went for some lunch on my side of the river, while the others got the boat back to pass out. The guys invited me to join them for dinner on their side of the river tonight. So I went home for a shit, shave and shower and got the boat across to join them. Fuck me do I regret not staying on this side, its beautiful. The countryside behind the guesthouse bamboo huts, were covered in rice paddies and banana plantations with such a hippy vibe within the village. Don't get me wrong my side was full of temples and amazing rock formations made by millions of years of volcanic activity and erosion. But instead of hippy backpackers, I had cows and monkeys.

Once we had dinner and watched the sunset, the guys said to me how was I planning to get back across the river as the last boat was about an hour ago. So in a panic I said by to the guys and ran to the riverbed, before the tiny bit of sunlight that was left, fucked off. By the time I got to the river it was pitch black and I had no torch. The only light I could see was coming from the top of the temple next to my guesthouse in the distance, so if I had to swim at least I know what direction to aim for. Luckily as I was sitting on a rock by the side of the river hoping the reflection from the stars on the water would not fade, some old Indian dude approached me. He said if I wanted to get across he would take me on his boat, so I jumped up with joy asking where he's boat was. He told me I was sitting on it, and what I thought was a rock, was in fact he's homemade boat, made from Bamboo and Banana leaves, I can only describe as a turtle shell upside down. Fuck me, at this point I was regretting not just swimming it. So we got in his turtle shell and started to paddle across. We got half way and the boat started filling up with water, he then told me to paddle faster, as if we was to take too long it would sink. I thought he was joking at first, but watching him panic with his paddle convinced me he was serious. We got across safe and sound, with this old man's turtle shell fishing boat, not at the bottom of the river bed. I give the guy some money not knowing what I gave him, as I could still not see a fucking thing. Then made a slow walk to the temple, which I could see lit up in the distance. It took me a while, but finally made it back to my guesthouse. Next time I go out for a sunset dinner, I'm taking arm bands.

My plan was to check out from here and go and join the guys on the hippy side for a few days, but when I got back, I started planning dates and places I still wanted to see, if my health improved. To be honest, I had three meals today without gagging, which is a massive improvement, so there and then I decided to keep heading north, and book myself a bus for the following day to Mumbai. The journey to Mumbai took roughly 16 hours, I had the bottom bunk on a sleeper bus, and I was the only white dude on this bus. So yes every Tom, Dick and Harry wanted to talk to me. I just love the Indian hospitality out here, constantly being fed. The bus stopped quite a few times, so people could have a piss, chai tea or dinner. Every time we stopped the Indians insisted on buying me tea or food, and as much as I refused, it seems they are offended if I say no. The majority of the time I'm communicating with hand gestures and facial expressions, as there English is so broken and I have no idea how to speak Hindi. So after a long journey and a good night's sleep, thanks to valium. I arrived in Mumbai at 7am, I got a tuk tuk to a guest house I was recommended by the crew in Hampi. It took me a while to find it, as again the driver did not speak English and could not read the map in my lonely planet.

I checked in and had a little nap (still high on Valium), and I was woken by a very familiar high pitched voice coming from reception, so I poked my head out my door to see Bolly standing there trying to check in. I could not believe it, what's the bloody chances, as much as I was trying to get her out of my head it was great to see her and know she was safe. She was in Mumbai for two days, like me, but was going to Hyderabad whereas I was moving north to Udaipur. We both met some cool people in this guest house and all did things together during the day sightseeing. Mumbai is not what I was expecting, because it was home to the biggest slum in Asia, I was expecting a complete shithole. However it was expensive, full of great architecture and had all sorts of western shops, Levi's, Reebok, McDonalds, the lot. Don't get me wrong, you still see people taking a shit on the side of the road, and it was covered in litter, but was nice in other ways.

When me, Bolly and three other girls took a tour round the city, I realised how polluted this place was. At first I thought the normal smell of human shit was making it hard to breathe, but it was the air pollution. I thought Bangkok was bad, but Mumbai is definitely the worst place I've been for it. Our last night we decided to go and watch a Bollywood movie, but 10 mins into it we all decided to leave as we wanted to see singing and dancing, not an action/comedy we couldn't understand, so we decided to go and get drunk. Bolly never come as she don't drink, so went home early with some dude she had been flirting with all night, whilst me and some Canadian chick and 2 birds from Israel went to a bar. We got talking to some Indians about any nightclubs in town, and was told there was one round the corner. So me and the two Israel's went, while Canada went home too tired. It was a very expensive but epic night. The next day me and Bolly went for a coffee and a chat about what we had done since we split up, and was nice to be friends having a normal convo. I had to board my bus a few hours later, to get a 20 hour bus ride to Udaipur, in Rajasthan. Another eventful journey full of weird conversations with broken English. At one of our stops, the guy in the restaurant see I wasn't eating, and asked if I wanted a beer, I was gobsmacked. As alcohol is hard to come by in India because of laws, religion and licences. So the dude came over to my table with a fosters can wrapped in newspaper and poured the beer under the table. It was jokes, I felt like I was in some drug deal, abit of a scary experience but a much needed beverage.

Fuckinnneeelllll booky boy, I think Rajasthan is gonna be a proper bit of me. I arrived in Udaipur roughly at 9am, and as stubborn as I am with tuk tuk's, rickshaws and taxis, I refused to get in one, as I convinced myself I knew where I was going. All I knew was that the bus station was somewhere east of the city, and the guesthouse I wanted was across a lake, somewhere west of the city. So trying to navigate by the sun, like a fucking tit, got myself lost in the slums of Udaipur. I was actually quite enjoying the experience of walking around lost in the slums, all the oldies kept inviting me in for tea, all the kids wanted to know my name and wouldn't shut up about fucking cricket. It was cool I felt very welcome. I finally decided to get myself a tuk tuk once some old woman begger with 7 seven fingers on each hand started touching me. I couldn't bloody believe it, I was only a few kilometres away from the lake, if it wasn't for Mrs more finger's no thumbs, I would have found it myself, still it was nice watching the tuk tuk man rub his hands together, when I gave him 50 rupee's.

When I finally got to my guesthouse I checked in and had some breakfast in its rooftop restaurant, and fuck me what a sight, Udaipur city is beautiful. It's built around a huge lake, with a massive palace bang in the middle surrounded by mountains with temples on each summit. All its very old buildings were at least 5 stories high and had roads which were more like alley ways, which could just about squeeze a car and a cow down them. My guest house was awesome, I met some pukka people who have been here a few days already, and given me some good tips of what to see. My first day I got a boat ride around the lake to see all the amazing buildings and temples Udaipur had to offer. I was going to jump in and have a little swim, as it's so fucking hot, until I see a group of people having a shit and washing there arse by some steps into the lake. There's all sorts of different house tunes coming from within the temples, I couldn't work out what was going on, but when I got back to my guesthouse the guys told me its Lord Shiva's birthday, so everyone is celebrating all day and into the night. Happy days, so me, two Swedish chicks, 1 Austrian dude and a guy from Bali with a cockney accent, got 'Dogs#!t' on the street carnival that night.

The next day me and Mimi (the guy from Bali who by the way has a cockney accent because he has been studying in London for the past 4 years). Decided to rent out some motorbikes and take a drive to one of the temples on top of one of the mountains. I'm not gonna lie we did get lost, but once we made it, it was worth it, we could see the whole city from up here, it was stunning. Plus the temple grounds were full of monkeys I've never seen before. They looked like albino orangatangs. When we got back we bumped into Austrian micky and went for a smoke down by the lake for sunset. I do like a good sunset, but it's so much better when your high, watching it over mountains, sitting on a spiritual lake, outside a 600 year old temple. When we got back we sat in our guesthouse and watched octopussy (James bond) on the big screen, which supposingly is something you need to do in Udaipur as octopussy was filmed in this city. The next day I got e-mails from the girls from Israel, telling me how cool Bundi was, and that I should meet them there. So fuck it I booked myself a train for later that afternoon. Micky and Mimi left that afternoon as well, which give me more reason to keep moving. They were really cool guys, and hope to see them both at the Holi festival, at the end of the month in Pushkar.

That last day in Udaipur, me and the Swedish girls took a tour round the royal palace, which was very interesting and learnt a lot about the history of the Sikh's, but cut the tour short, because to be honest got bored and just wanted to get stonned for my train journey to Bundi. I'm a little bit worried about this next trip, because my train arrives in Kota at 11pm and I have to get a local bus, if there still running half an hour down the road to Bundi. Then hope to god I can find a tuk tuk that knows where the guesthouse is, where the Israeli girls are staying, fingers bloody crossed.

Well what a fucking mission that journey was I got on my train and sat next to some Indian dude, who told me the train stops at Bundi, so there's no need to go to Kota and get a bus. As much as this old dude had terrible English, I ended up talking to him about random shit for 2 hours, we had some dinner (good old fashioned Thali), then decided to have a few hours' sleep. This old boy was going to Bundi as well, and told me not to worry he would wake me, if I'm asleep when we get to Bundi. Still not having a phone, watch or alarm clock, left all my trust in this man. Well, it was me who woke him up, once we had gone past our stop, and ended up in Kota. I was so pissed off, I would have stayed awake if I knew this old guy was as unorganised as me. We got off the train and he was on the phone to his wife, who was shouting down the phone at him, because she was standing outside Bundi train station. After his stressful phone call he told me he was going to sleep on the floor and wait for the morning train back, there was no way in hell I was willing to do that. I haven't seen a white person on the train or at this very busy train station, so I decided to find a cheap guest house till morning.

When I walked out of the station, the taxi and rickshaw drivers come at me like fly's round shit, I managed to pick a happy face from the pack of wolves and started to way up my options, he tried telling me he would take me to bundi in his tuk tuk, for 1000 rupees, but made no sense as its cheaper for me to find a guest house and grab a train back in the morning so I told him if he could find me a bottle shop, and a cheap guesthouse, I would be a happy man. So we drove to a stall on the side of the road selling beer, and we both sat in his tuk tuk talking shit having a drink, it was then he turned around and said he would take me to bundi for 500 rupees. So fuck it I bought us some beers for the drive, and went on this hour road trip to Bundi. The roads were fucked, pot holes everywhere, and was pitch black, it was 1am the driver was a fucking nutcase, he had Indian music blaring out full blast, speeding round at oncoming trucks. It was a pukka experience, well worth the 10 dollars it cost. I finally arrived at the guesthouse, where Yael and Hadar were staying to find the doors were locked. So my driver banged on the doors till he woke someone up to let me in, the Indian guy he woke was not best pleased, but was happy to see me as he was expecting me.

I woke up in the morning to the Israeli girls in my room jumping on my bed, hugging me as they stayed up late worrying something had happened, as it was there last day in Bundi, they had a plan for us to go and explore some waterfalls, so the 3 of us shared a tuk tuk and drove on roads similar to last night, about 40k down the road to a canyon. The drive was amazing, we drove through the countryside passing tiny farming villages. Every Indian kid we see, was so happy to shout out hello, and wave to us, some of the poorest but happiest people in the world. The canyon was fucking awesome, dry season, so not much of a waterfall, but still an amazing climb down to the river below which was full of monkeys and mongoose. We was hoping it was going to be a peaceful few hours, but half way down the canyon, was a temple, and it was Ganesh's birthday, (Hindu elephant god), so there were a lot of Indians celebrating. When we got back to Bundi we went for dinner and met some cool English dude called Rupert. So after dinner me Rupert and the girls went back to my room, as my room was fucking massive, and started playing some drinking games. Unfortunately for Rupert, he had to leave at 11pm, because our guesthouse locks the front door. Fortunately for me and the girls, we all stay in the same guest house, therefore continued to get 'Dogs#!t' till early hours.

I woke up the next morning with a banging headache, and my room trashed to bits, to discover the girls out in the garden restaurant, having breakfast looking fresh as daisies. They had to check out at 10am, so must have set an alarm, where I slept like a baby right through till 11.30, best nights kip I've had since oz. We decided to take a walk to a lake with a temple, which was cool, it had a lot of history, and some amazing art, but I think my temple days are done. On the way to the lake, loads of kids kept asking us for pens, so on our way back, I bought a pack of pens, and handed them out, like some sort of god. It was awesome, they were so happy. Why have I been giving the beggers money, from now on everyone is getting a pen. We got back to the guesthouse and said goodbuy to the girls, not for long as we arranged to meet again in Pushkar next week for the Holi festival. Everyone I meet is going Pushkar for the Holi festival, it's going to be sick.

That night I bumped into Rupert and two English girls and joined them for a few drinks in some funky café, but was shattered and didn't want to be locked out because of my 11pm curfew, so had an early one. The next day I took a walk to see parts of bundi I've not seen, like the palace and the fort. I've never been Scotland but it reminds me of Edinburgh, the town is in the middle of these huge hills with castle walls to make up the fort and a huge palace that looks over the whole town, truly amazing! But fucking hard work getting up and down them bloody hills. I got back to town and decided to book myself a train to Rathambore national park for the following day, really need to keep moving, got less than two weeks till I fly to Amsterdam, and still so much I want to see. I went and had dinner that night on a rooftop café and met a couple from Switzerland who look like the biggest stonners I've seen, both with dreadlocks and red eye, and I was right as soon as I finished eating, they pulled out a chillum. I tried to refuse, as my experience smoking a chillum in Goa, fucked me up. But 'Tommy no limits' cracked on and not long after was in need of a spoon with my pillow back in my room. I was actually quite happy to have an early night with a good night's sleep as I was checking out the next day.

I checked out and went and had one more chai tea with all my Indian friends who worked in random shops up and down the street and am now sitting here in my favourite café, with free Wi-Fi. The Israeli girls have messaged me saying they want to meet me in Jasaimer which is where I'm going after the national park. Fuck knows why, it's not like I put in much of a performance that night, but sometimes two minute Tommy is all a girl needs. What a fucking mad couple of days it's been, I boarded my train to Sawai Madhopur which is a town next to the tiger reserve and believe it or not I actually managed to stay awake and get off the right stop. However the train got there at 1am so another eventful journey in a tuk tuk in the dark was in order. I walked out of the station and asked some dude to take me to a cheap guest house close to the national park. Clearly the guy listened to every word I said and drove me to a 5 star hotel.

They tried charging me 1500 rupees, and when I refused dropped it down to 1000 rupees, if I wasn't so tired I would have kept looking, but this place had hot water and a proper mattress with no piss stains on the sheets. So fuck it I thought I would treat myself. I had a word with the guy at reception about booking a safari in the park, he told me there were morning and evening safaris, and that he would wake me up at 5am to get to the booking office to book one. But in desperate need of a good night's sleep, I told him not to wake me up, and that I would book an evening tour myself, but as great listeners as the Indians are got woken up at 5am with a tuk tuk waiting outside to take me to the booking office, great 3 hours sleep and I'm up and out booking safari's. Determined to get back to bed I thought I would go and just book myself an evening safari, so I could get back and make love to the mattress. This booking office wasn't your average walk through, is was like the train stations, with shit loads of people in, no cues just one big free for all, on a first come first serve basis. I was still half asleep and freezing my fucking nuts off, surrounded by all kinds of funky smells coming from all these arguing Indians. In the middle of this mosh pit, I spotted two westerners, and had half a shouted conversation about the kaos going on. These safaris are done in 4x4/16 seaters called canters, and 6 seaters called gypsies. The guys were telling me that you needed a group ready yourself to book a spot, not like your average organisation that would just take booking and stick any tom, dick or harry together, oh no this is India, and that's far too easy. So Simon the English guy and his missus Jessica from California, invited me to jump on a gypsie with them and 3 other Indians. So I gave Jessica my money and thought I would fuck off down the road for a chai tea, while the guys sorted it out. I got back to see Jess had not moved position in this fucked up cue, and see Simon standing on the edge of the crowd. I said to Simon isn't that meant to be your job to stand and cue for tickets in the middle of a shit load of smelly blokes, but he reckons his missus takes no shit and gets the job done. He wasn't wrong either, she was pushing and elbowing all the Indians to get to the front, it was jokes.

Once we got our tickets, I realised I was now going on the morning safari, fuck it after watching what Jess had just been through I was grateful to be on the safari at all. I was not prepared for the tour, I was wearing no warm clothes, and the sun was still yet to rise but luckily Simon had a spare jacket. It was an awesome tour, unfortunately didn't see any tigers, but got to see leopards, spotted deer, samba deer, antelope, and all kinds of different birds including vultures. Rathombore national park has such an amazing landscape, it proper felt like I was in Africa. Once I got back to my hotel, I went to the train station to book my ticket to Jasaimer, where I was planning to meet back up with the Israeli girls. So I had my train booked that evening for 7pm. I got back to my hotel to discover Simon and Jessica in the reception waiting for me, they were going back to the national park for an evening tour and asked if I wanted to come? Determined to see a tiger I tagged along knowing the tour finished at 6pm, which give me enough time to catch my train.

Our gypsie 4x4 involved Me, Simon, Jessica, a guy from Germany, and 3 German girls. Our driver had been told about tigers being spotted in a different part of the park, the same morning. So we took his advice and went to 'zone 9'. Our morning tour went to 'zone 6', which was cool, but didn't see shit in this place. The landscape here was so much more diverse, we drove over sand dunes, through rivers, up and down canyons, and through some awesome local villages. I got to see all the same wildlife as I see in the morning, plus Sloth Bears, Panthers and a Hyena. We sat by a lake watching the sunset, hoping to see a tiger, but no luck, a bit gutted, but was so worth going back on an evening tour. The sunset was beautiful and I wasn't freezing my nuts off. The drive back was jokes, we stopped in the first village at a bottle shop, and bought a load of beers, our driver who was drinking with us was blasting out Indian tunes all the way home. We got back around 8pm, so yes I missed my train, oh fuck it I was quite happy I stayed an extra night. So we stopped off at my hotel to pick up my stuff and checked into the guest house all the guys were staying in. We finished off our beers and all went for a local Thali, the food was amazing, and the home made whisky was interesting but done the job.

The next day we woke up and had breakfast together, then me and Simon went to the train station to book our tickets out of here. Everything was fully booked to Jasaimer, but I had an option to get a train to Jaipur, then get a bus to Jasaimer, so this was my new plan. So I got a rickshaw back to the guesthouse grabbed my shit and rushed back to the train station as it was leaving in 20 minutes. I said bye to the guys, sweating my nuts off, arrived on my platform to discover the train delayed one hour. Fucking India, nothing is simple. So I sat on the platform for an hour, and got stared at by everyone, as I was the only white man in sight. It was only a two hour journey, so I bought myself a general ticket, which is the cheapest class to get, and fuck me will not be doing that again. The carriage was so busy, people getting on and off through the doors and windows. Women and children were being thrown all over the place, it was complete kaos. I managed to squeeze myself into the corridor on the carriage and sat on the floor, everyone was staring and blatantly talking about me. Normally I get half a broken English conversation out of someone, but no-one could talk English. I did get passed on a spliff which was nice, but the most awkward and most uncomfortable two hours of my life.

I arrived in Jaipur and rushed around for somewhere to book a bus to Jasaimer. I found a booking office not far from the station and the guy told me the bus leaves in half an hour from the other side of the city, so very confused about what he said, I stood there like a tit in a trance, wondering if I had just been stitched up. But then this random bloke pulled up on his motorbike and told me to jump on. It was fucking hard work trying to hold on with my backpack on my back, guitar in one hand and hand luggage in the other, but got to my bus with time to spare to have a beer in the pub next to the bus stand. I have no idea how this bus made its 14 hour trip to jasaimer, it looked and sounded like it was going to fall apart. Nevertheless I arrived safe and sound to this amazing city. The city is built around a huge fort, which is now residential, full of restaurants, guesthouses and old temples. I was on my way into the fort, as I was told a good place to stay by the German girls from the safari. But got convinced to stay in a guest house just outside the fort for a hundred rupees a night, with free Wi-Fi and a swimming pool. So I phoned Yael and Hadar and told them the name of the guest house as I reserved a room for them. After a well needed shower and some breakfast met the girls in reception, and took a wander around the fort trying to find the cheapest way to do the camel safari across the desert. As we were temple trekking around the fort we bumped into Santiago from Columbia.

The girls had met the guy in Jodpur the day before and he had already booked his safari for the following day at a really good price. So we decided to book the same tour. That evening me, Santiago, and the girls went for a meal and was planning to go back to ours for a pool party, but because of the 11pm curfew, the guesthouses have, Santiago had to get back, plus all the shops were closed to get any booze once we realised we had none. It was probably for the best as we had to be ready for 8pm for the 3 day camel safari.

Holy fucking testical Tuesday, I'm only back in good old blighty, before I tell you how miserable, grey, wet and dam right 'Dogs#!t' the weather is, let me tell ya the amazing end to my 2 and half year trip. So me and the Israeli girls squeezed into a 4x4 with Santiago, Ida the Danish girl, Noa another Israeli, and a South African couple. We drove about 40k to the place where we met our camels. My camel's name was Mr Magoo, and boy was he a trooper. Me and Magoo were first to be packed, strapped and ready to ride. So we started trotting off without the others. The Indian tour guides were shouting to me that I needed to head left towards a tiny village in the distance, but this is the first time I've been on a camel, I don't know how to steer it, I mean it doesn't even have indicators. However it didn't take long to figure out. I had a rope in each hand, one pulled it left, and the other went right, I know, I know it's not rocket science but it would have been nice to have been told.

What an amazing feeling it was to be out in the desert, just me and magoo and nothing in sight, but sand and a few gazelles running about. I was pleased to have purchased my bright orange turban that was wrapped around my head and face, because fuck me it was hot. After a few hours ride, we pulled up in a village, population of about 20, and all had to get off our camels and walk them through the village, it's a sign of respect, to walk through instead of riding. The children in this village were the cutest little devils I've ever met. Normally the children in India beg for stuff, but oh no not desert kids, they just take. My turban was my savour, the kids kept their distance from me, pointing calling me a guru. I even asked one kid to give the bracelet he stole back from Noa and he did, hell fucking yes ginger god 1-desert child 0. Once we got through the village and escaped with our lives from the 10 year old demons, we rode a few more hours to a place we all had lunch in the shade under a tree.

It was nice to sit down and finally meet the group properly, plus my ass needed a rest from the pounding from Mr Magoo. The tour guides done an excellent job, making chai teas and our veg thali's. We played a few games of cards and had a little jam with our newly formed band. Me and Noa had Guitars, Yael had a Keyboard Harmonica and Santiago had a Tabla. I loved it, we proper looked the part, shame we sounded like pots and pans hung from a tree in a hurricane, 'all the gear, no idea'. Once our tour guides rounded up all our camels, we ventured further west towards the sand dunes. It took a few more hours to get to the dunes, we were camping on that night. What an amazing spot to set up camp for sunset. Truly mesmerising sight. When I say 'set up camp', I mean the blankets we were sitting on the camels, were put on the floor for us to sleep on and the camp fire was lit for us to see each other and keep warm. As we were all sitting round the camp fire singing songs from our home countries, a random man appeared from the darkness with a bag full of cold beers, fuck me it was desert Santa clause. These beers were double the price, but went down a treat, 'desert Santa you are a legend and will not be forgotten'. It was truly an unforgettable evening. Our tour guides were singing us traditional Indian love songs, as well as made up piss takes of western songs. My favourite was the Barbie song, but instead of Barbie girl it was desert man.

The next morning we woke up for sun rise, which was just as beautiful as the sunset, and unfortunately had to say by to the

South African couple, as they were only on a two day tour. Luckily me, Santiago, and the girls had another night, so we rode further into the desert toward the Pakistani boarders. We rode for hours, before coming to our lunch destination under another big tree. It was here I wrote a song that me and Scotty will be singing at my brother's wedding in May, hopefully. After another delicious, 'very meatless' lunch, we all rode to our night time place to camp. This ride was more of a trot, as I think we were running late, however still arrived at our desert dune camp for another sunset. Once we enjoyed the amazing and very tranquil sunset, we had a dinner which involved anything that was still edible, which, trust me, it wasn't much. So all sitting round in a circle chatting away, still very hungry and now bored of sand and stars, our saviour came from beyond the dunes, Mr desert Santa. I'm starting to think it's not desert Santa, and that this guy has done this before, but still, couldn't give a fuck, the man has got cold beer. When we first arrived at our dune camp, we noticed a shit load more, fat dune bugs or dung beetles, or whatever the politically correct name is for these guys. There basically them big black beetles that just seem to push poo around all day. Well when the sun was up, it was easy to push them away, now its pitch black, I'm freaking out, as I have no idea where the fuckers are so I put on all the clothes I had, spooned up to the guys as close as possible, closed my eyes, I hoped I would be there in the morning, not getting rolled down a hill by the gang of bugs roaming the desert for giant ginger human shaped poo's.

Success it was, I didn't get mistaken for poo, instead was in the same position I went to bed in, being woken up for breakfast. We had breakfast but didn't touch the sides what so ever and trotted on to our final village where our 4x4 was waiting to take us home. It had been an awesome few days, but was in desperate need of a good meal and a shower. Me and the guys went for a good meal but didn't make it a late one, as we needed to check out in the morning. As me and the girls was getting a bus to Pushkar the following afternoon. We checked out and had a good walk around the Jaisalmer fort, I love this town, it's a very beautiful and clean part of India. Me and the girls had a very weird lunch on a rooftop restaurant in forty degree heat with hail stones the size of jack Russell dogs. Then finally boarded the bus of death to Pushkar.

I got on the bus to find my bed was pissed wet through, as a window was left open, when we had a cloud of jack Russell's roll over. So the girls kindly let me share their double bed, bless them, as it was a night bus and sleep is something I'm in need of. Now in India, they overload public transport more than anywhere I've ever been, but this particular bus was a joke. I didn't realise how bad it was until we stopped at a place for a toilet break. There were more people on top of the bus, than there was inside it. Poor fuckers, it was pissing down as well. I almost felt sorry for them, knowing I was dry inside having an Israel's sandwich. Once we squeezed back onto the bus through a corridor of pervy sweaty India men and up to our bed, we managed to get a few hours sleep before arriving in Pushkar. We arrived early hours in the morning, so had to sleep in a communal room/kitchen/reception before our rooms become available.

My first day involved in eating a lot and getting the camel poo smell out of my clothes. I didn't really venture out of the hostel this day, which was good because I got to meet all the people that already live here. They all love getting 'Dogs#!t', happy days. The holi festival is in a few day's time. So everyone is in high spirits, and beings that Pushkar is one of the best places in India to celebrate it, I am looking forward to getting 'Dogs#!t' with everyone. The new friends I've made seem to know of a bottle shop not far from the hostel, so no desert Santa will be required. I had a few days in Pushkar to do a bit of shopping and get ready for the day of carnage to come. The holi festival has conveniently fell on the day before my flight to Amsterdam, and Im planning to spend the holi festival a few hundred kilometres away from Delhi airport. This could work out to be a very smart move or I could end up being a bigger Muppet than I thought. I am a big fan of Pushkar, It's a beautiful city I've never seen so many colours (apart from one night in mushroom mountain but that's another story).

I just can't get my head around how much more colourful it will be once the paint fight kicks off. In case you didn't know, booky my old mukka, holi festival celebrates its historic story by a mass water and fluorescent coloured powder paint fight. Every night leading up to the festival, everyone in town congregated down by the town square to dance around in a massive circle while a dozen Indian guys played tabla and a few other instruments on podiums/tables in the middle. It felt like I was a part of a new tribe, it was awesome. I bumped into quite a few friendly faces in Pushkar most of whom I had met in India, but a few from Thailand, too. We always invited everyone back to our guest house, as it's where the party was at. Love that guest house, every morning I would wake up, step out my door and see the most breath taking view over a lake that as surrounded by temples. The owners were so nice and polite, and cooked my eggs in the morning just how I like them. The day before the festival we went and got ammo for the fight. I treated myself to a huge water gun, water balloons, a few kilos of powder paint some glasses that I could shoot water out of and a bottle of whisky.

The night before holi, was the night of the full moon, so it pretty much kicked off that night. Me and my newly acquired army of international backpackers, played all sorts of drinking games on the rooftop of our guest house then ventured down to the town square. Everyone on this night danced around a huge bonfire instead of a band, but the sound of drums was still pumping. We had heard through the grapevine that the paint fights started early in the morning, so if I wanted a good spot in the square before it become packed, was to either stay awake and go right through or have an early one. Knowing I needed to be on that flight to Amsterdam, went and got a few hours kip. I got woken up in the morning to a monkey fight outside my door, the fucking annoying little shits. However done me a favour as I didn't have an alarm. I had to get ready and run my luggage across town to a bus depot, where I was meeting my taxi in the afternoon. I had to do this because the taxi would not be able to drive in town through thousands of multi coloured piss heads. I got back to the guest house in time for a few drinking games before we all went down to the square. It did seem a bit silly drinking so early knowing I still had to get half way across India that night, but fuck it its Holi fest and getting 'Dogs#!t' is on the cards. We had heard a few stories about women being groped and touched by locals in the crowds of the paint fight. Therefore the walk to the square was a funny one as all us guys formed a huge circle protecting the girls in the middle.

We made it to the square completely covered in paint. I was wearing a plain white outfit, as I wanted to see the full effects from the paint. However only being on the square for a few minutes, had my top ripped from my body. There was an electric cable running above our heads, which now looked like a washing line, as every blokes tops had been ripped off them and thrown over it. It freaked me out a bit, being stripped by the locals but once I had notice every guy without a top, it didn't bother me so much. What an amazing street party it was. The music was some of the best electronic I've heard, and to be half naked, covered in paint, and dancing with some of the coolest people I've met, was like I had died and gone to a backpacker's heaven. It got to about two pm and I had to say farewell to the crew as I had a taxi waiting.

The taxi made it to the station in record time. Every person that caught their eyes on me, pissed themselves laughing. By this point all the colours had merged on my face and body, and because the purple being so strong, I was now a Barney the bear lookalike. I waited at the station for a few hours, and in this time must had had my picture taken a hundred times. After a long uncomfortable train journey, I got to Delhi with a few hours to spare until my flight. I got a taxi straight to the airport as there was no way in hell I was missing my flight. I really wanted to stay in my multi-coloured clothes, however when I got to the airport and noticed there were showers, changed my mind. After nearly scrubbing the skin off my face, I give up and just had to deal with the fact I'm now purple and probably will be for the duration of my time in Amsterdam.

I checked in and went to look for a spot to chill till the gates opened. It was then I bumped into Bolly and Mitch.

I knew I would be seeing Bolly here as we booked this flight together a few months back, however seeing Mitch was a lovely surprise. He remembered us talking about how cheap this flight was, as we was flying with the second worst airline in the World, and decided to jump on the bandwagon. Unfortunately when we changed planes in Moscow he was going elsewhere, still, it was lovely to see his foot was better and in good health. Me and Bolly didn't actually get talking until we arrived in Holland as we were on different seats. The whole flight I was preparing a speech for Bolly to let her know how much deep down I hated her for breaking my heart and fucking up the end of my travels by getting balls deep with that cockhead a month ago. However once we got our luggage and walked outside, I had bigger problems in mind. I was wearing flip flops and it was snowing. Bright purple as I was, just wanted to get off the street and into a shower.

Divvy bolllocks Bolly hadn't booked any place to stay, and was an Amsterdam virgin, so we went to the place I had booked to get me checked in, so I could then show her a cheaper option. When we arrived at reception the guy informed me, that I had been upgraded to a room with a double bed as the hotel wasn't busy. As much as I wanted it to myself, knew that Bolly only needed a place for one night as her friends from home was arriving the next day, therefore offered her to stay with me. A few hours ago I was going to tell her, how much I think she is a poisonous little rat and now I am letting her share my bed, fuck my life booky boy, I need to grow some balls. It was actually quite a nice evening, talking about the end of our trip in India over a few joints of Amsterdam's finest. We both had an early one, enjoying the luxuries of hot water and a comfy bed the hotel had to offer. Bolly had to be up and out early to meet her friends and sister at the airport, I treated myself to a lie in as my friend Lewis wasn't due to arrive till the afternoon. When I finally crawled out of my pit I went shopping for some warmer Western clothes, as all I really had was summer surf wear or bright coloured Indian linen. I was really starting to feel uncomfortable with the amount of stares I was getting for being purple. I couldn't wait to get back and have another shower before I met Bolly's friends. I dread to think what she told them about me and being bright purple is just more ammo for them to take the piss. By the time they all arrived, I was not only purple but red through scrubbing in the shower so much. Luckily it was only a brief meeting in a café over a few joints. Lovely couple of girls if you ask me, shame we won't become friends, as this will probably be mine and Bolly's final goodbye.

When they left the café I had a few more big fat heads (spliffs) and got on a train to meet Lewis at the airport. It was so good to see him, not only because he's my best mate and I miss him, but he had more warm clothes for me, happy fucking days. My friend Lewis is a bit of a weed entrepreneur, and he has visited Amsterdam more times than he has London. So I let him take me to the best cafes with the best weed and for the rest of the weekend we were complete zombies, it was great. Unfortunately me and Lew had different flights home and although it's only an hours flight from Amsterdam to Southend felt like the longest flight yet I was already a bit freaked out by the cold weather and the fast pace of the Western world, but to think I was going back to a country even colder and faster, full of people who love to moan and queue was getting to me. My head was full of questions. Mainly, where the fuck did those two and a half years go. I miss Australia, Asia, the Tropics and cheap good food, but most of all I miss my family and good old Blighty. I know deep down my travelling days are not over, and with the trip I've just had, I will be content and happy until I set off again. I've got a great English summer to look forward to, a stag weekend in Newcastle and a wedding in Cyprus in just a few week's time. So booky boy, here's a big thank you for keeping me sane and making me feel like I had someone by my side the whole time, even though I pretty much did, cheers ta, with a little bit more cheers.

ATTENTION ALL GUESTS STAYING IN #202

WE WILL NOT ALLOW PARTIES TO CONTINUE IN THIS ROOM.

DUE TO A NUMBER OF COMPLIANTS IN REGARDS TO NOISE.

WE ARE NOW GIVING YOU A FIRST AND FINAL WARNING.

IF CAUGHT WITH LARGE GROUPS OF PEOPLE IN THE ROOM OR IF EXCESSIVE NOISE IS MADE **WE WILL EVICT THE ENTIRE DORM.**

WE ASK THAT YOU PLEASE RESPECT OTHER GUESTS STAYING IN THE HOSTEL, AND KEEP NOISE TO A MINIMUM, ESPECIALLY AFTER 10PM.

THANK YOU FOR YOU CO-OPERATION

NOAHS MANAGEMENT

Lightning Source UK Ltd.
Milton Keynes UK
UKOW05f0021260214

227145UK00002B/28/P